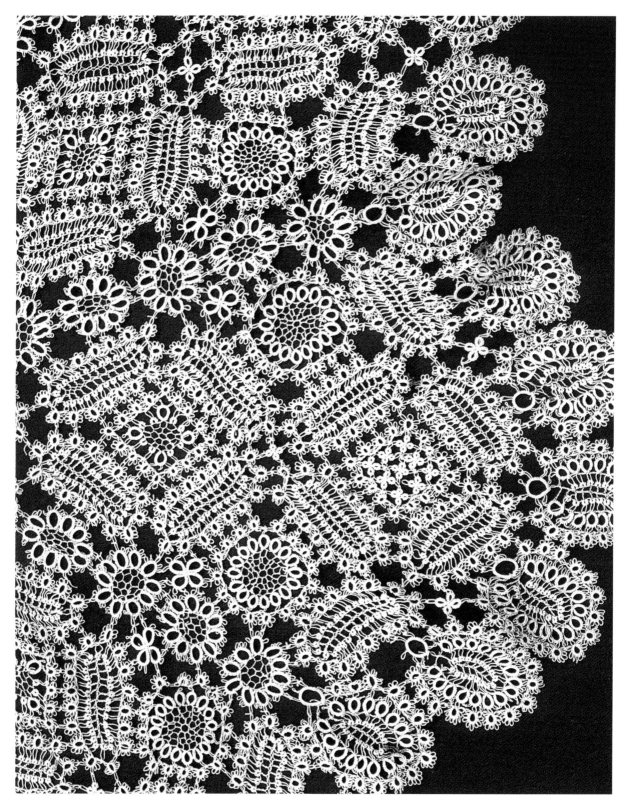

Photo 1 Tatting from a nineteenth-century parasol cover

TATTING
with
VISUAL
PATTERNS

Mary Konior

B T BATSFORD LIMITED • LONDON

Cover Illustrations:

Patterns designed and worked by the
author using pearl cottons, embroidery
threads and oil paint.
Front - "Carnival" (pg 48)
Back - "Lilac" (pg 102)

First published 1992
First paperback edition 2002
©Mary Konior, 1992

A CIP catalogue record for this book is available from the
British Library.

Typset by Goodfellow & Egan, Cambridge
and printed in Singapore by Kyodo Printing Co.Ltd

for the publishers

B T Batsford
64 Brewery Road
London N7 9NT

ISBN 0 7134 8802 6

CONTENTS

Photo 74 *Shuttles old and new*

INTRODUCTION

I have often sung the praises of tatting, but must admit to being upstaged by a farmer's wife from Devon, who once reduced a class to chaos by announcing, 'I like tatting because I can put it in my pocket when I go to feed the pigs.' To my shame, I have forgotten her name, or I might now be prodding her for a pithy comment on visual tatting patterns.

The main advantage of a visual or diagrammatic system is that it enables tatters to understand directions at a glance, rather than having to read, painstakingly, every written word. This is surely a contribution, albeit a small one, to speed in tatting, and as such it should be welcome.

To those who are not familiar with the visual presentation of patterns, there is nothing new in their use. Continental and Japanese publications have used them for many years. They eliminate language barriers. However, there is no standard form.

Many tatters evolve their own systems of visual notation, but not everyone finds another's system easy to follow. I have been asked occasionally to 'please write it out properly', and suspect that some systems are over-simplified and reduced to a minimal form which bears little relation to the actual tatting.

For this reason, my aim has been to lay out each diagram so that it relates as clearly as possible to the structure of the tatting whilst, at the same time, providing sufficient information regarding stitch counts and sequence of work. General written notes are included where further directions are necessary, for instance where difficult joins occur.

Clear photographs are an important part of a visual system and can be regarded as auxiliary 'diagrams'. The majority here are given full size or in an enlarged version. For even 'more clarity, it may be useful to keep a magnifying glass within reach. A magnifier may also, of course, reveal an occasional imperfection in workmanship – something which no self-respecting author would wish to have revealed – so it should be used only sparingly as a last resort! It is a pity that enlargement detracts from the delicacy of the work, but experienced tatters will know that tatting always looks prettier on a small scale, and that the finer the thread, the more beguiling the effect.

The threads used in this collection are Coats *Chain Mercer Crochet*, DMC *Cordonnet Spécial* and DMC *Fil à Dentelles* (now re-named as *Spécial Dentelles*), with an anonymous assortment of pearl cottons and other embroidery threads in the pictorial work. The size of thread for each design is given merely as a guide to measurements; there is no reason why size should not be changed at the worker's discretion.

This publication is intended as a practical workbook, and therefore a number of technical tips are included where appropriate in the KNOW-HOW boxes. As some of these tips may also be useful in a different context, readers are recommended to browse through all the KNOW-HOW boxes before embarking on a project. More basic techniques are given at the end of the book.

The patterns have been chosen to cover a wide range of skills. There are designs for the fully experienced, adventurous tatter, for the tentative novice, and for all grades in between. The easiest patterns, suitable for novices, are marked with a dagger (†).

The following standard abbreviations are used wherever a written explanation accompanies a diagram:

ds double stitch
hs half stitch
Jk Josephine knot
p picot
rw reverse work

HOW TO WORK FROM THE DIAGRAMS

—————
A single shuttled thread (as when working rings)

—————
A second thread (as when working chains)

- - - - -
A space of unused thread

0 0
Picots

● ●
Josephine knots

- An arrow indicates the general direction of work.
- The number of double stitches relative to each position is given in figures.
- Where letters of the alphabet are used, they indicate the sequence of work.
- A numeral set in a circle identifies the sequence of rows or rounds where relevant.
- Any further notation will be explained with the relevant pattern.
- The need to reverse work should be apparent from the lay out of the diagrams.

The following diagrams are given with equivalent written directions in order to explain the system.

Diag. 1

Ring of (4ds, p) 3 times, 4ds. Space. Ring of 4ds, join to last picot of preceding ring, (4ds, p) twice, 4ds.

Diag. 2

Ring of (4ds, p) 3 times, 4ds; rw. Chain of 6ds, p, 6ds; rw. Ring of 4ds, join to last picot of preceding ring, (4ds, p) twice, 4ds.

THE PATTERN COLLECTION

BRAIDS
AND
PANELS

Anniversary

Using Coats *Chain Mercer Crochet* No. 20, the single braid measures 22 mm (⅞ in) in width, the double braid measures 3 cm (1¼ in). A matching motif is given on page 80.

Single braid

Start at A with a centre ring of (3ds, p) 7 times, 3ds; rw. Continue from the diagram for the length required. All joins to the centre rings are made with the shuttle thread.

Double braid

Turn the single braid upside-down and turn the diagram similarly. Continue along the other side as shown.

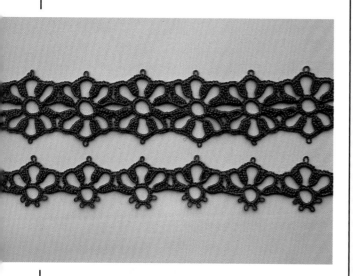

Photo 2 Anniversary

KNOW-HOW 1

To join tatting with the shuttle thread

This is a fixed join which does not slide like a normal tatted join. It is commonly used when working a series of chains, where a normal join would cause the work to twist.

To make a shuttle-thread join, insert the hook into a picot, catch the shuttle thread and pull it out into a loop. Pass the shuttle through the loop and position and tighten the resultant knot. As this is a fixed knot, be careful that it does not tighten before it has been positioned accurately.

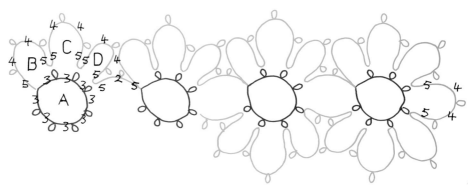

Diag. 3

Beaded Braid

Using Coats *Chain Mercer Crochet* No. 20, the tatting measures 2 cm (¾ in) in width. Rocaille beads are threaded on the ball thread before working the first row. The positions of the beads are indicated on the diagram by black circles.

1st row

Start at A with a ring of (4ds, p) 3 times, 4ds; rw. Continue from the diagram, slipping a bead into position between each of the chains as shown.

2nd row

Turn the 1st row upside-down and work in the opposite direction. All joins on this row are made with the shuttle thread.

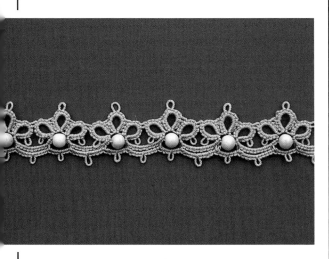

Photo 3 Beaded Braid

KNOW-HOW 2

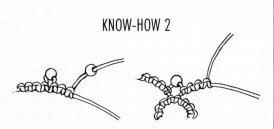

Figs 1(a) & (b) Adding beads to tatting

To add beads to tatting

There are several methods of adding beads to tatting but the most practical way is to thread them on the ball thread before starting work. Each bead is then brought into position when required. A small bead (or cluster of beads) looks well when placed on a picot (a), or when placed between chains (b). If different colours or different types of beads are used, any relevant sequence should be planned in advance, and the beads threaded in reverse order of requirement.

It is often inconvenient to thread beads on the shuttle thread as they tend to impede work, but beads can be added to all-ring tatting if each is slipped onto a joining picot before the join is made. A short length of fine wire can be inserted through the picot to make the task easier, and the picot must be long enough to take the hook after the bead is added.

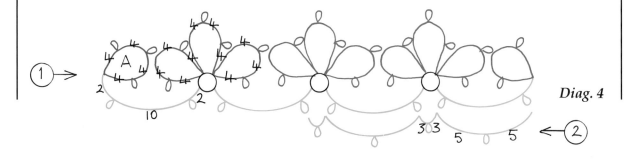

Diag. 4

Black Magic

Using DMC *Cordonnet Spécial* No. 40, the panel measures 38 mm (1½ in) in width and length is adjustable. A short piece makes a very good bookmark.

Start at A with a ring of (3ds, p) 7 times,

3ds; rw and continue from the diagram. All chain-to-ring joins are made with the shuttle thread. Chain-to-chain joins are normal joins. Where a chain joins to a small ring, make a minimal picot over the join.

Work completely around the final ring, thus turning the tatting upside-down. Turn the diagram similarly.

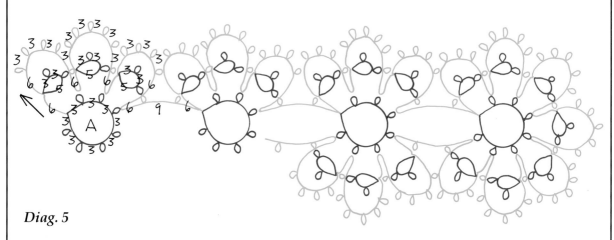

Diag. 5

Photo 4 Black Magic

Crooked Mile[†]

Using Coats *Chain Mercer Crochet* No. 20, the tatting measures 2.5 cm (1 in) in width.

All rings are worked alike; only their joins and orientation vary.

Start at A with a ring of 5ds, p, (2ds, p) twice, 5ds; rw. Continue from the diagram, leaving minimal spaces between rings A to F, and no spaces at all between rings F to M.

Diag. 6

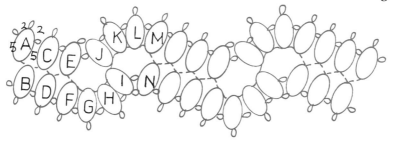

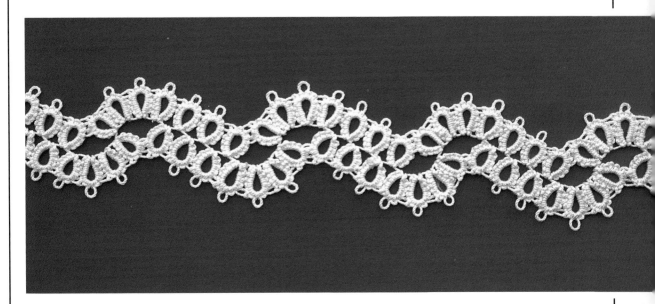

Photo 5 *Crooked Mile*

Curds and Whey

Using Coats *Chain Mercer Crochet* No. 40, the tatting measures 2 cm (¾ in) in width.

Start at A with a large ring of (3ds, p) 7 times, 3ds; rw. Small ring of 4ds, (p, 2ds) 4 times. Join the shuttle thread to the last picot of the large ring and continue from the diagram, leaving minimal spaces between the rings and the joins. Only reverse work after every large ring.

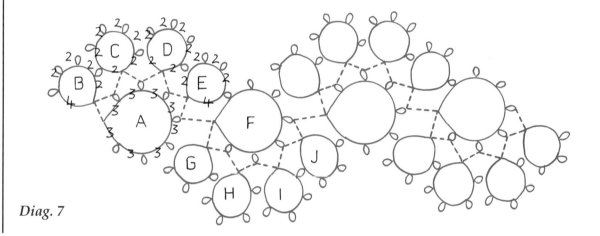

Diag. 7

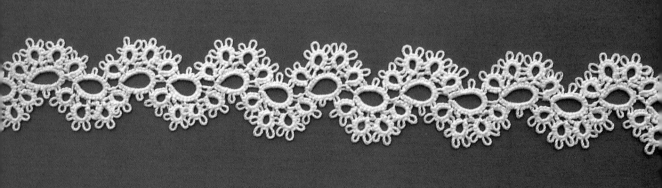

Photo 6 Curds and Whey

Duet

Using Coats *Chain Mercer Crochet* No. 20, the double row measures 4.5 cm (1¾ in) in width. A single row also makes a useful braid.

1st row
Start at A with a small ring of (4ds, p) twice, 4ds; rw. Continue from the diagram, leaving minimal spaces between the rings. All small rings are alike and all large rings are alike.

2nd row
Start at A and join to the 1st row as shown.

Photo 8 *Doll's dress trimmed with single rows of Duet; hat trimmed with Honesty. The doll is from an edition sculpted and made by June Gale of the British Doll Artists' Association*

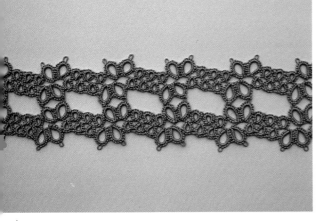

Photo 7 *Duet*

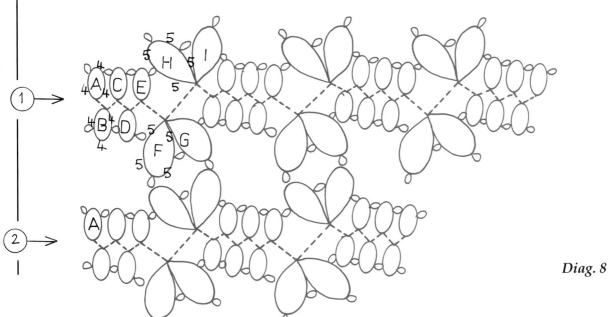

Diag. 8

Filet Panel

This panel was adapted from a filet-crochet design, which suggests that many other filet-crochet designs could similarly be transformed into tatting.

Using Coats *Chain Mercer Crochet* No. 60, the tatting measures 5 cm (2 in) in width.

Start from the bottom left-hand corner of diagram 9, working lock stitch to form a false picot. Continue the foundation chain with (8ds, p) 6 times 8ds; rw.

1st row

Chain of (2ds, p) twice, 6ds, p, 4ds, join shuttle thread to last picot of foundation chain, * 4ds, join to previous picot of 1st row, 6ds, p, 4ds, join shuttle thread to next picot of foundation chain. Repeat from * to end of row; turn.

Continue from the diagram(s), turning work at the end of every row. Notice that all rings face downwards. Diagram 10 represents half the panel.

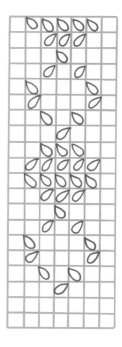

Diag. 10

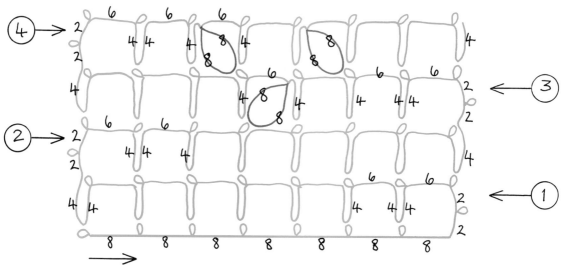

Diag. 9

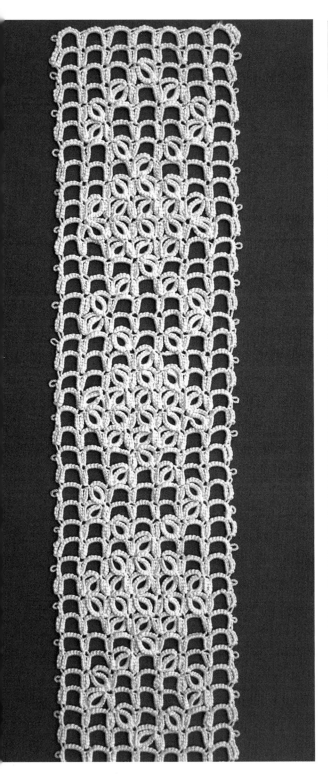

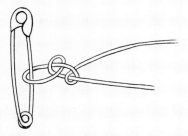

KNOW-HOW 3

Fig. 2 Forming a false picot with lock stitch

To commence a chain with lock stitch
Lock stitch is used to prevent a stitch from running on the shuttle thread. It is useful for stabilizing work when a pattern starts with a chain.

With the shuttle wound directly from the ball, hang a safety-pin on the thread, in order to give your fingers something easy to hold. Work a lock stitch, thus forming a tiny loop (which can be regarded as a false picot) around the safety-pin, and continue the chain as usual.

To work lock stitch make a first half stitch, but omit the transfer of the loop, thus making an incorrect half stitch (sometimes called a 'reverse stitch'). Follow it with a correctly worked second half stitch, and the two together have locked the threads as shown.

Photo 9 Filet Panel

Jack and Jill†

Using Coats *Chain Mercer Crochet* No. 20, the tatting measures 38 mm (1½ in) in width.

All rings are worked alike; only their joins and orientation vary. Start at A with a ring of 6ds, p, (2ds, p) twice, 6ds; rw. Continue from the diagram, without leaving spaces between the rings.

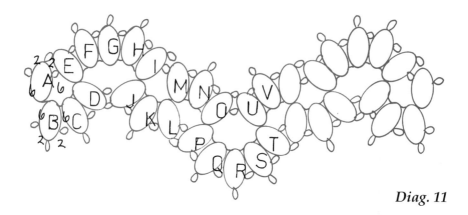

Diag. 11

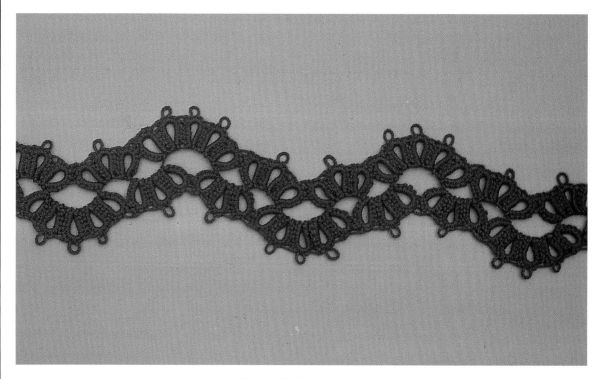

***Photo 10** Jack and Jill*

Photo 11 *Jack and Jill worked in pearl cotton and mounted on gathered fabric to simulate smocking*

Leaf Braid[†]

This is the easiest pattern in the book and probably the most useful!

Using Coats *Chain Mercer Crochet* No. 20, the tatting measures 2 cm (¾ in) in width, and will ease to a curve.

Start at A with a ring of (4ds, p) 3 times, 4ds. Continue from the diagram, leaving a minimal space every time work is reversed.

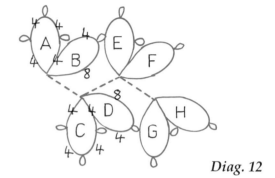

Diag. 12

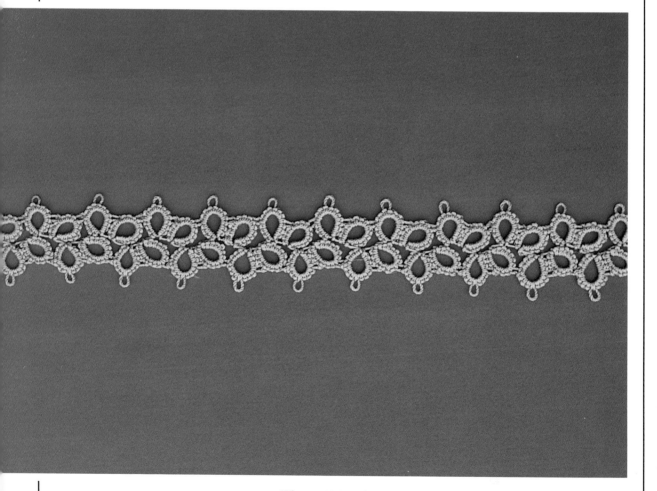

Photo 12 Leaf Braid

Lupins

This is an example of roll tatting.

Using Coats *Chain Mercer Crochet* No. 20, it measures 2.5 cm (1 in) in width, and will ease to a curve.

Roll stitches are indicated on the diagram as a double line. Start at A with a ring of 2ds, p, 1ds, 30 roll stitches, 1ds, p, 7ds. Notice that '1ds, 30 roll stitches, 1ds' is given as 30R on the diagram. Leave a minimal space every time work is reversed.

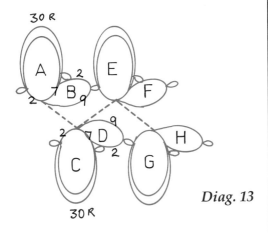

Diag. 13

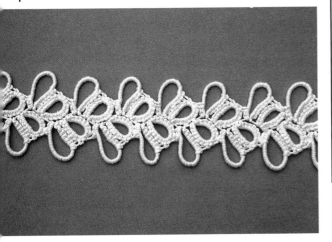

Photo 13 Lupins *(see enlargement p. 109)*

KNOW-HOW 4

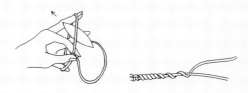

Figs 3(a) & (b) Roll tatting

To work roll tatting
This has a cord-like appearance, which makes a good contrast when used in conjunction with normal tatting.

To make a ring in roll tatting, start in the usual way and work at least one normal double stitch, then work a roll stitch by passing the shuttle upwards through the ring, as shown in (a). Tighten the shuttle thread so that the roll transfers to the ring thread, and continue to work roll stitches, as shown in (b). Keep them well under control with the thumb, as they have a perverse tendency to become unrolled. Finish the ring with at least one double stitch before closing it. These double stitches are not absolutely necessary, but they make it easier to control the tatting.

Work a double stitch before and after each picot, in order to separate it from the roll stitches. Similarly, work double stitches before and after each join.

Merry Wives

Using DMC *Cordonnet Spécial* No. 40, the tatting measures 2.5 cm (1 in) at its widest, and will ease to a curve.

Start at A with a ring of 5ds, p, (2ds, p) 4 times, 7ds. Continue from the diagram for the length required. The first chain connects to ring D with a shuttle-thread join.

Diag. 14

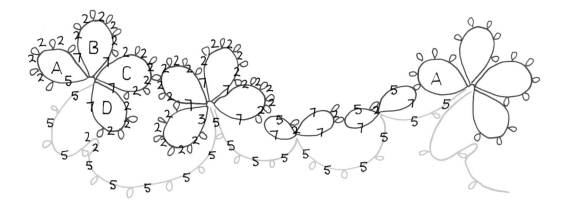

Photo 14 *Merry Wives*

KNOW-HOW 5

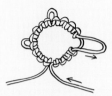

Fig. 4 Opening a closed ring

To open a closed ring

Most tatters admit defeat at this manoeuvre, as once a ring is closed any attempt to open it again by pulling at its base will only tighten the last stitch, so making the task impossible. However, a closed ring can be opened by easing the stitches apart elsewhere on its circumference, at a picot, and gently pulling the running thread revealed there, with a fine crochet hook, or with tweezers.

Continue to pull in the direction shown until more thread has been loosened and then the stitches can be shunted along until the loosened thread appears at the base of the ring. The ring can then be fully opened and each stitch unpicked one by one, as required.

Photo 15 *Merry Wives with a shuttle of abalone shell*

Midnight

Using DMC *Cordonnet Spécial* No. 40, the bookmark measures 3.5 cm (1⅜ in) in width.

All rings are worked alike; only their orientation varies. Leave a 10 cm (4 in) length of thread at the beginning.

1st row
Start at A with a ring of 6ds, p, (2ds, p) twice, 6ds. Continue from the diagram for the length required, ending with a group of three rings to match the beginning. Cut, leaving a length of thread as before.

2nd row
Work to match the 1st row, joining the two rows as shown.

For the tassels, cut 6 to 8 threads 20 cm (8 in) long, for each tassel, fold in half, and attach them with a hook. The threads left on the tatting should be pulled through the nearest tassel. Trim the tassel ends neatly.

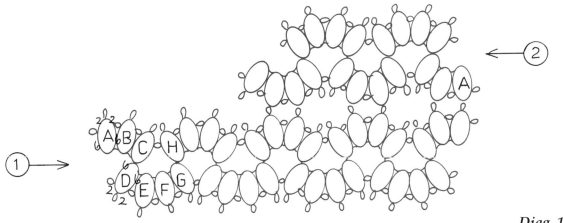

Diag. 15

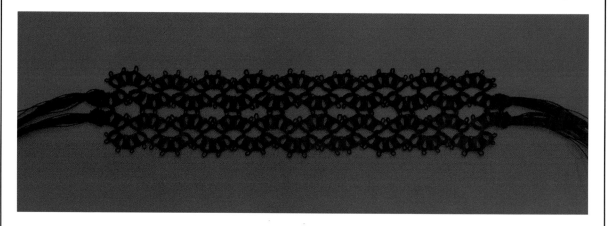

Photo 16 Midnight

Mischief

Using DMC *Fil à Dentelles*, the bookmark measures 4.5 cm (1¾ in) width. Two shuttles are required, wound on a continuous thread.

Start at A with a ring of (3ds, p) 5 times, 3ds; rw, and continue from the diagram.

Chains are joined to rings A, B, F and G by the shuttle thread. All inner rings are the same size. All outer rings are the same size. Change shuttles for the outer rings, and for the Josephine knots, as indicated by the colours. Each Josephine knot consists of 10hs.

Attach tassels as instructed for **Midnight** (opposite).

Photo 17 *Mischief*

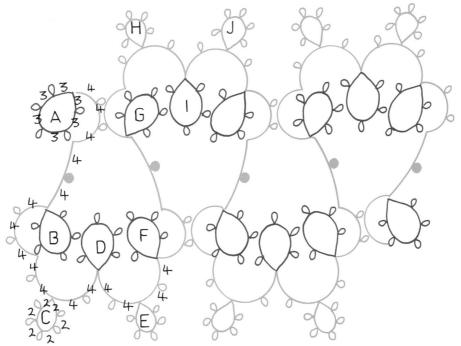

Diag. 16

Onion Skins

Using Coats *Chain Mercer Crochet* No. 20, the braid measures 2.5 cm (1 in) in width, and will ease to a curve.

Start at A with a ring of 10ds, p, (1ds, p) twice, 10ds; rw. Continue from the diagram, reversing work between chains D and E, E and F, and so on. All joins are made with the shuttle thread except where chain H joins chain E. When joining to the base of a ring (where there is no picot), insert the hook between the most convenient threads.

Photo 18 Onion Skins (see enlargement p. 110)

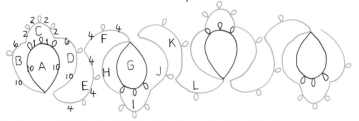

Diag. 17

KNOW-HOW 6

Fig. 5 Overlapping threads

To renew a thread by overlapping
This is the quickest way to renew a thread, and it can be used to replace a shuttle or ball thread. It is best worked at the beginning of a ring or chain. It gives a slight thickening where the threads are doubled so, in order to compensate for this, fewer stitches need be worked than given in the pattern. Picots should

not be worked with the double thread.

For a chain, overlap the old and new ball threads sufficiently to wrap the whole overlap on the left hand, around the fourth finger, clutching tightly. Work three or four double stitches, then drop the old thread and continue with the new. For a ring, overlap the old and new shuttle threads sufficiently for both to encircle the hand completely, again clutching tightly, and proceed as given for the chain. Ends can be clipped once the ring is closed, or once the chain is completed.

Skipping Ropes

Using Coats *Chain Mercer Crochet* No. 20, the braid measures 2 cm (¾ in) in width, and will ease to a curve.

This design is worked entirely in chains, one advantage being that the shuttle seldom needs refilling. See KNOW-HOW 3 (p. 15) for starting with a chain.

Start at A with a false picot, 5ds, p, 7ds, p, 12 ds, join shuttle thread to false picot in order to form a false ring; rw. Continue in chains from the diagram, reversing work after every false ring. All joins are shuttle-thread joins, with the exception of those between E and H, H and I, I and J, and J and A, which are normal joins.

Photo 19 Skipping Ropes

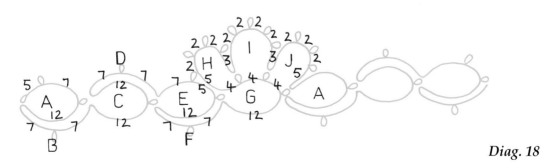

Diag. 18

Photo 20 From a wedding veil trimmed with
Skipping Ropes in No. 60 crochet cotton. The
inner row is a simplified version of the pattern

EDGINGS
WITH
CORNERS

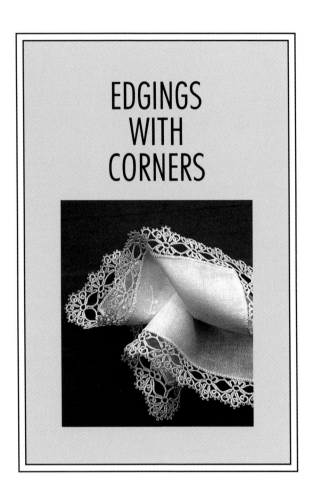

Asters

Using Coats *Chain Mercer Crochet* No. 40, the edging measures 2.5 cm (1 in) in width, and will ease to a curve.

Start at A with a ring of 5ds, p, 3ds, p, 8ds; rw, and continue from the diagram. The chain joins to ring E by the shuttle thread.

Photo 21 *Asters*

Photo 22 *Handkerchief showing Asters worked in DMC* Fil à Dentelles.
The fabric is hemmed with double-crochet, as explained in
KNOW-HOW 15 (p. 75)

KNOW-HOW 7

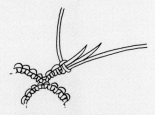

Fig. 6 Concealing ends

To conceal the ends of a knot
Hide the two ends by 'weaving' or running them alongside the shuttle thread so that they are hidden inside a few double stitches. This should be done at the beginning of a ring or chain.

If the ends in question are short, the manoeuvre can be more easily achieved by using a hook to pull both ends through each half stitch before the latter is positioned and tightened.

When it is feasible to plan the join well in advance, some tatters prefer to leave longer ends, and thread them, together, through a needle, which is then slipped through each half stitch as required.

Alternatively, each end can be treated separately, running one into a chain, and the other into a ring, although of course this involves twice as much work.

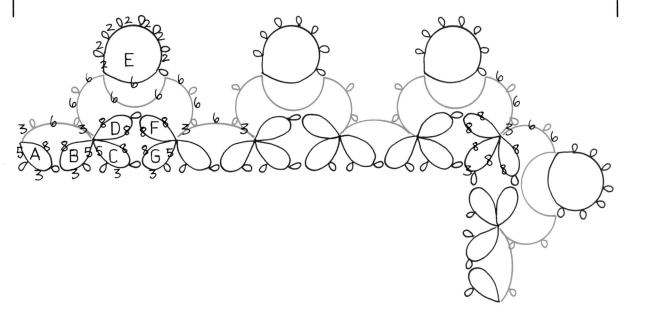

Diag. 19

Babylace[†]

Using Coats *Chain Mercer Crochet* No. 40, the edging measures 2 cm (¾ in) in width.

Start at A with a ring of (3ds, p) 5 times, 6ds. Ring B of 6ds, join to last picot of ring A, (3ds, p) 4 times, 3ds; rw and continue from the diagram.

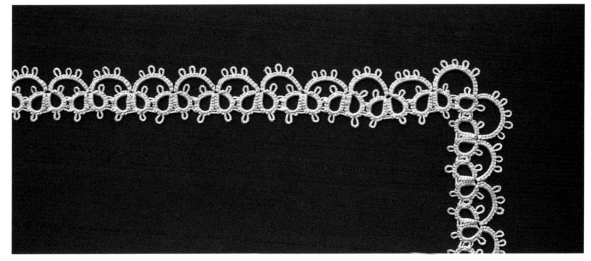

Photo 23 Babylace

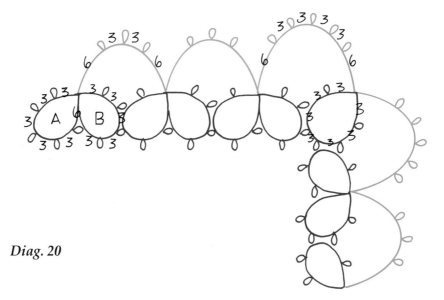

Diag. 20

Beauty Spots

Using Coats *Chain Mercer Crochet* No. 40, the edging measures 22 mm (⅞ in) in width, and will ease to a curve. Josephine knots are sometimes known as beauty spots.

Start at A with a ring of 4ds, p, 7ds, p, 4ds, p, 7ds. Work rings B and C from the diagram, then take the shuttle thread to the back of the work and join it to the picot which connects rings B and C. Work ring D. Bring the shuttle thread back and join it at the base between rings B and C.

Work ring E from the diagram. Leave a minimal space and work a Josephine knot of 10 hs. Join the shuttle thread to the centre picot of ring E, so that the Josephine knot is enclosed within the ring. Leave a minimal space and make a similar Josephine knot before working the next ring A, which encloses this knot as it joins to ring E. Continue from the diagram as shown.

Photo 24 *Beauty Spots*

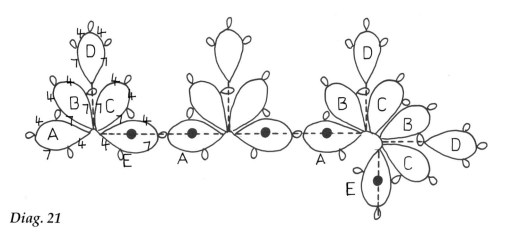

Diag. 21

Bo Peep

Using Coats *Chain Mercer Crochet* No. 60, the edging measures 3 cm (1¼ in) in width.

First work the small corner motif separately. Then start the edging at A with a ring of (4ds, p) 3 times, 4ds; rw, and continue from the diagram. All rings are the same size; all large chains are the same size; all small chains are the same size. Join to the corner motif as shown.

KNOW-HOW 8

  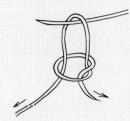

Figs 7(a), (b) & (c) Making a weaver's knot

To tie threads with a weaver's knot (or sheet-bend)
This knot is especially useful if a disastrous break has occurred because it can be manipulated with as little as 6 mm (¼ in) of thread protruding from the tatting. It is also a knot which can be positioned accurately, wherever required.

Make a loose slip-knot with the new thread, as shown in (a) and (b). Pass the loop of the slip-knot over the broken end, and tighten the slip-knot carefully by pulling in both directions, (c). The loop of the slip-knot should gradually disappear, drawing the broken end into the knot where it should turn and become securely embedded.

Sometimes a second attempt is needed before the end turns and becomes properly embedded. If it is merely enclosed without turning, it will slip out. Test for security by tugging the new thread before continuing work.

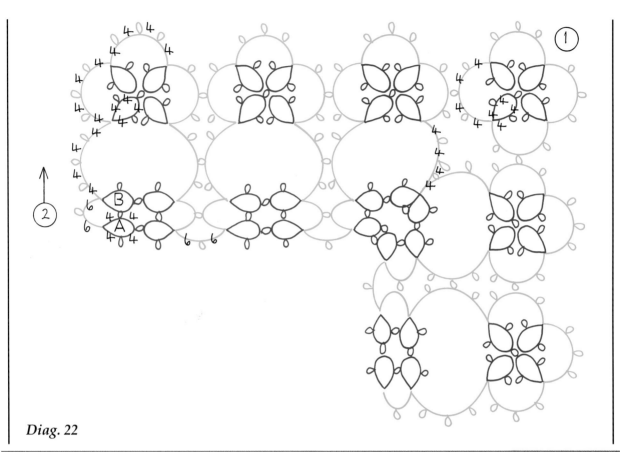

Diag. 22

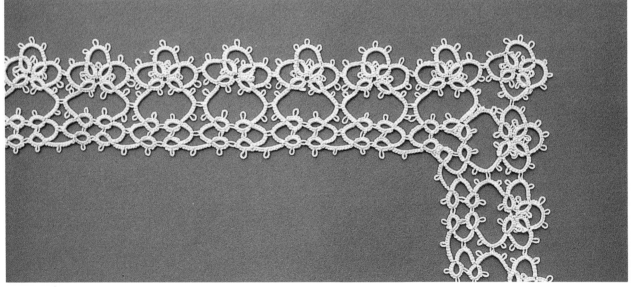

Photo 25 Bo-Peep

Bridesmaids

Using Coats *Chain Mercer Crochet* No. 60, the edging measures 3 cm (1¼ in) in width.

1st (inner) row

Start at A with a ring of (4ds, p) twice, 1ds, (p, 4ds) twice; rw. Continue from the diagram as shown. Rings A, B and C are alike.

2nd (outer) row

(using the shuttle thread only)
First work the corner ring separately. Tie to ring E and without leaving a space, work corner ring F of 3ds, join to ring D, (3ds, p) 7 times, 3ds; fasten off.

Start again, with ring G of (3ds, p) twice, 3ds, join to the inner row as shown, 3ds,

join again to the inner row, 2ds, (p, 5ds) twice; rw and continue from the diagram. All outer rings are alike, and all small rings are alike. Leave minimal spaces between rings G to O. The size of space between ring O and the following ring G is up to you.

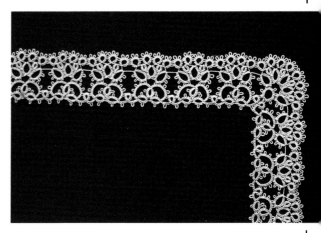

Photo 26 Bridesmaids

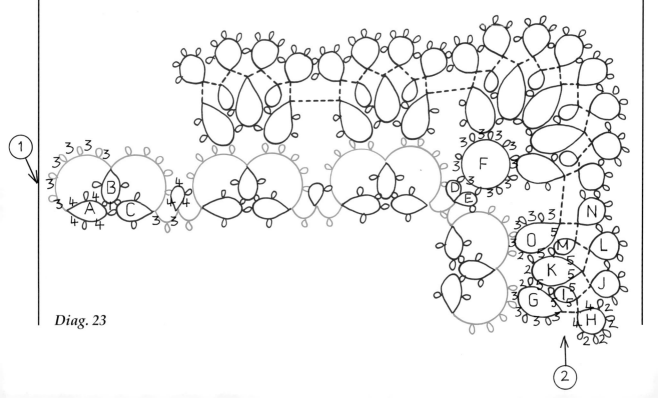

Diag. 23

Chain Reaction

Using Coats *Chain Mercer Crochet* No. 40, the edging measures 2 cm (¾ in) in width, and will ease to a curve.

This design is worked entirely in chains, one advantage being that the shuttle seldom needs refilling. See KNOW-HOW 3 (p. 15) for starting with a chain.

Start at A with a false picot and continue in chains from the diagram. All joins are made with the shuttle thread. Reverse work after every join except after chains D and F.

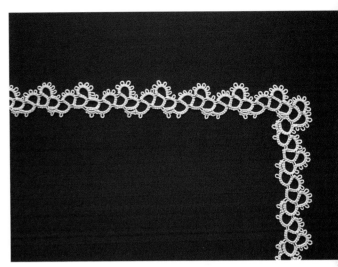

Photo 27 Chain Reaction

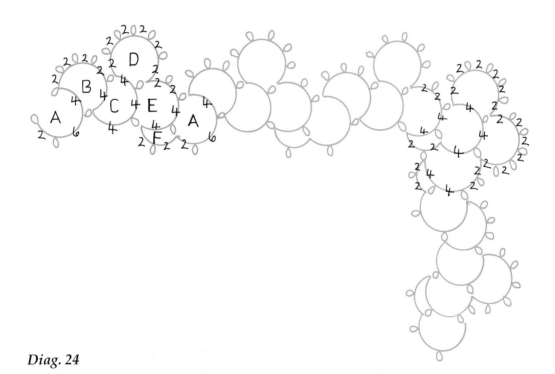

Diag. 24

Clover

Using Coats *Chain Mercer Crochet* No. 40, the edging measures 2 cm (¾ in) in width, and will ease to a curve.

Start at A with a ring of 5ds, p, 3ds, p, 8ds; rw, and continue from the diagram. The chain joins to ring D with the shuttle thread, and the corner chain joins to the extra corner ring similarly.

Photo 28 *Clover*

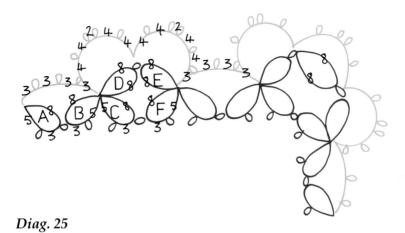

Diag. 25

KNOW-HOW 9

Fig. 8 Renewing a ball thread

To renew a ball thread
It is not strictly necessary to tie a knot when renewing a ball thread.

Instead, conceal the loose end of new thread A by running it inside the first few stitches of the nearest ring, and conceal the loose end of old thread B in the following chain. Both ends will be safely anchored, and can be clipped once the chain is completed.

Do not attempt this loose-end technique when renewing a shuttle thread, or the work may pull apart.

Eternity Rings

Using Coats *Chain Mercer Crochet* No. 40, the edging measures 3 cm (1¼ in) in width.

1st (inner) row
Start at A with a ring of (6ds, p) twice, 12ds; rw. Chain of 6ds, p, 2ds, p, 6ds, join shuttle thread to last picot of ring; rw, and continue from the diagram. Each chain in this row is joined to its horizontal ring by the shuttle thread. The corner 'ring' is a false ring, made with a chain.

2nd (outer) row
Start at E with a ring of 4ds, p, 2ds, p, 6ds, p, 3ds, p, 9ds; rw. Chain of 3ds, join to 1st row as shown, 2ds, join again to 1st row, 6ds, join shuttle thread to ring E, and continue from the diagram.

Photo 29 Eternity Rings

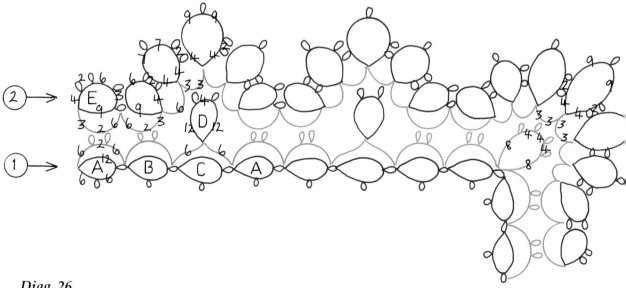

Diag. 26

Gossip

Using Coats *Chain Mercer Crochet* No. 40, the edging measures 1.5 cm (⅝ in) in width.

1st (inner) row
Start at A with a ring of 2ds, p, (3ds, p) twice, 2ds, p, 10ds; rw. Continue from the diagram as shown. All chain-to-ring joins are made with the shuttle thread. All chain-to-chain joins are normal joins.

2nd (outer) row
All joins are made with the shuttle thread.

Photo 30 Gossip

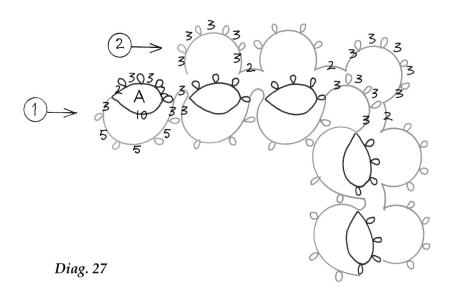

Diag. 27

Honesty†

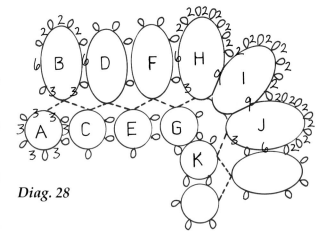

Using Coats *Chain Mercer Crochet* No. 60, the edging measures 2 cm (¾ in) in width.

Start at A with a small ring of (3ds, p) 5 times, 3ds; rw.

Continue from the diagram, leaving a minimal space every time work is reversed.

Diag. 28

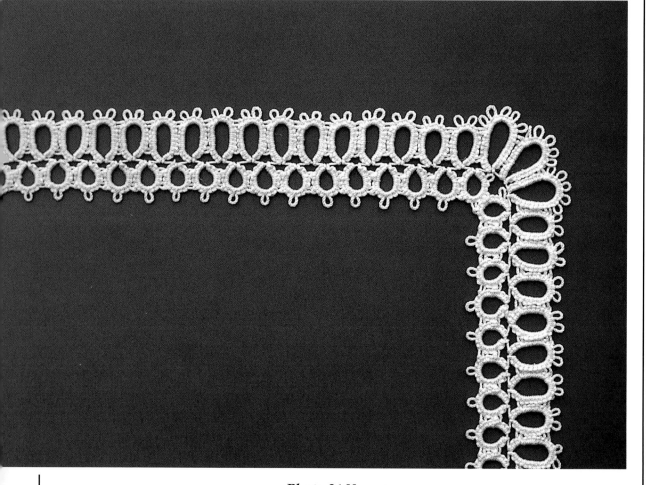

Photo 31 Honesty

Maids of Honour

Using Coats *Chain Mercer Crochet* No. 60, the edging measures 2.5 cm (1 in) in width. Work the outer row first.

1st (outer) row
Start at A with a large ring of 2ds, p, (3ds, p) 3 times, 2ds, (p, 3ds) 3 times; rw.

Continue from the diagram as shown. All chain-to-ring joins are made with the shuttle thread. All chain-to-chain joins are normal joins. Where a chain joins to a small ring, make a minimal picot over the join.

2nd (inner) row
Work in the opposite direction as shown. All chain-to-ring joins are made with the shuttle thread. All chain-to-chain joins are normal joins.

Photo 32 *Maids of Honour*

Photo 33 *A handkerchief edged with Maids of Honour in* DMC Fil à Dentelles. *The fabric is hemmed with double-crochet, as explained in KNOW-HOW 15 (p. 75)*

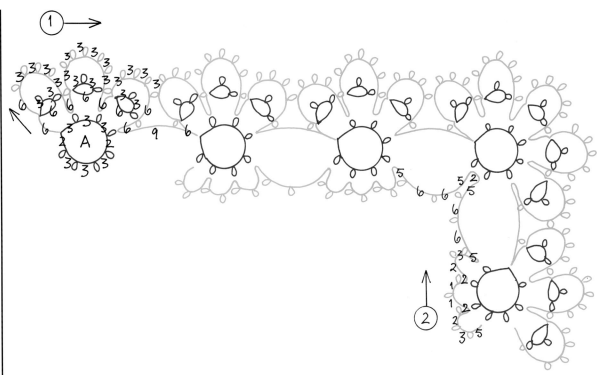

Diag. 29

KNOW-HOW 10

To make a twisted bar
This consists of an extra-long picot which is afterwards twisted when needed for a join.

Because twisting will shorten a picot it is best to experiment first in order to assess the exact length which will be required. When joining, insert a hook into the picot and twist several times before finishing the join in the usual way.

If working a series of matching twisted bars, cut a small piece of cardboard as a gauge for measuring the length of each picot. Give the same number of twists to each when joining.

Wallflowers

Using Coats *Chain Mercer Crochet* No. 40, the edging measures 28 mm (1⅛ in) in width.

This design includes twisted bars (*see* KNOW-HOW 10 p. 43), which are shown on the diagram as straight lines.

Start at A with a ring of 5ds, p, 3ds, p, 8ds; rw. Continue from the diagram, twisting the long picots into bars as explained. All chain-to-ring joins are made with the shuttle thread. All chain-to-chain joins are normal joins. Make an extra-long corner bar.

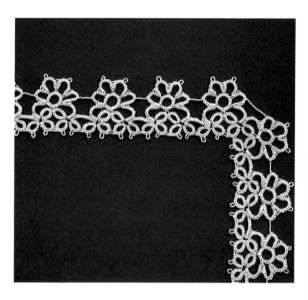

Photo 34 Wallflowers (see enlargement p. 111)

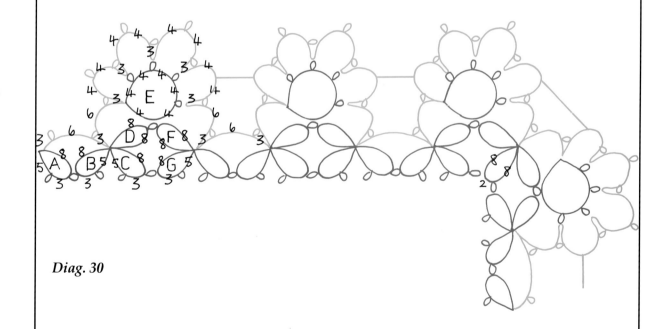

Diag. 30

ACCESSORIES
FOR DRESS
AND TABLE

Bell Flower

Using Coats *Chain Mercer Crochet* No. 40, the flower measures approximately 6.5 cm (2½ in) in diameter when assembled. Fine floristry wire and floristry tape are needed; artificial stamens are optional.

Bell motif (make 3 for each flower)
With the shuttle wound directly from the ball, start at A with a centre ring of (2ds, p) 8 times, 2ds; rw.

Continue from the diagram, working all around the centre ring. All chain-to-ring joins are worked with the shuttle thread.

Make a minimal picot over these joins, except when joining to the centre ring. Chain-to-chain joins are normal joins.

To complete the motif, join to the base of ring C and ring B when working the last chain, using the method for connecting a rosette, given in KNOW-HOW 14 (p. 70). Tie the end of this chain to the centre ring.

To assemble the flower
Wire each bell motif separately, running fine floristry wire through the base of the motifs and twisting to form a stem. If stamens are used, they are enclosed in a fold of doubled wire. Place three motifs together and wrap the combined stem with floristry tape.

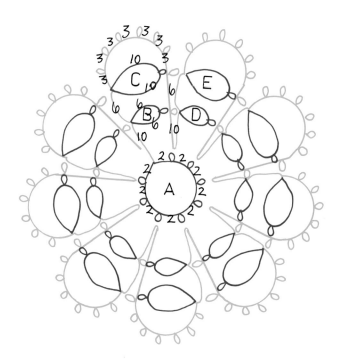

Diag. 31

Photo 35 *Bell Flower*

KNOW-HOW 11

To assess thread requirements
When working a series of repeating motifs, it saves thread, and effort, if the exact length can be wound on the shuttle each time. To assess the amount needed, wind the shuttle with a known length, work the first motif, and then measure the thread left unused. The difference between the original length and the thread left unused is the length required.

There is no need to measure in centimetres or inches; use the traditional armstretch instead.

Carnival

Using Coats *Chain Mercer Crochet* No. 20, each motif measures 6.5 cm (2½ in) in diameter.

Start at A with a ring of 4ds, p, 3ds, p, 7ds; rw. Chain of 7ds, p, 11ds, p, 2ds, p, 2ds; rw. Continue from the diagram as shown.

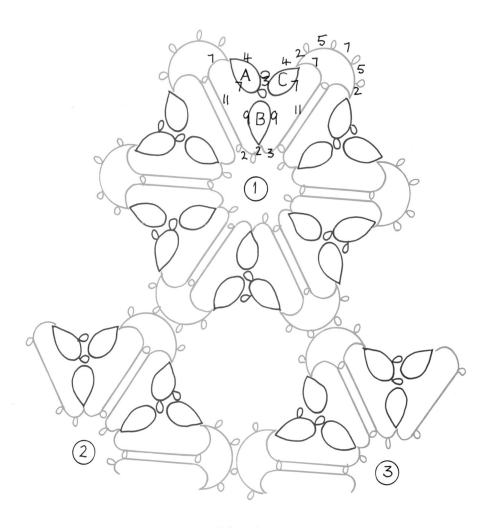

Diag. 32

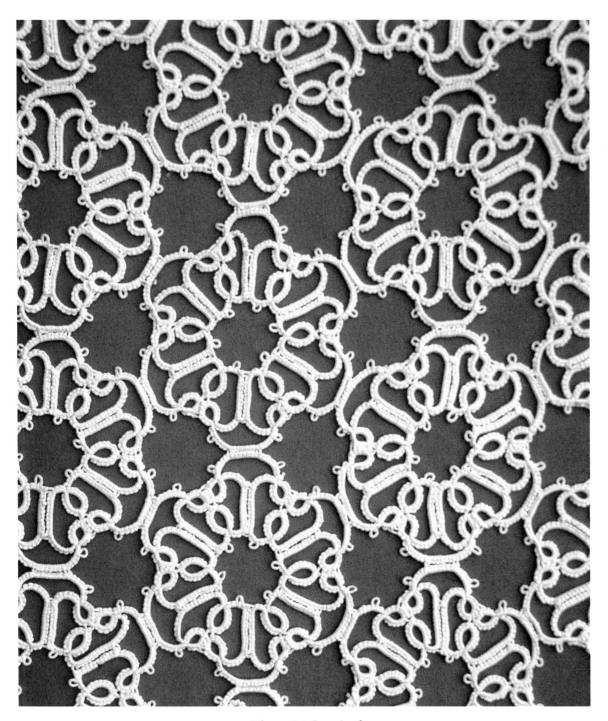

Photo 36 *Carnival*

Crescent Collar

This is an example of random or irregular tatting sometimes called free tatting. Anyone who has not attempted random work before is advised to begin with a smaller project, such as the coasters shown on page 84, before attempting a collar.

Using Coats *Chain Mercer Crochet* No. 20, the collar shown measures approximately 9.5 cm (3¾ in) in width at the centre front, and 43 cm (17 in) in length at the inner edge, but size and shape are adaptable. Draft and cut a paper pattern of the exact dimensions needed, and mark approximate positions for the flower fragments, which are worked first.

Flower fragment

This is worked in two parts. Start at A with a ring of 4ds, p, (2ds, p) 4 times, 6ds, and continue from the diagram. Leave ends of thread on each chain, and tie to the corresponding junctions of rings C and D. Work three flower fragments all together, then work two separate flower heads. Set aside until needed.

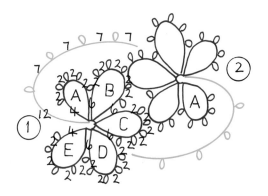

Diag. 33

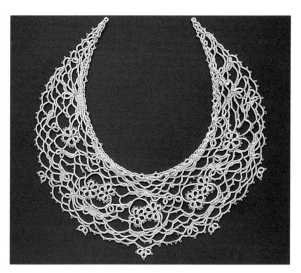

Photo 37 Crescent Collar

Inner edging

This is a foundation row which is not apparent in the illustration because it has been folded back underneath the collar. Start with a * ring of (4ds, p) 3 times, 4ds; take the shuttle thread across the back of the ring and join to the centre picot. Repeat from * for the length required.

Random tatting

Exact directions are not given for the random work as it would be inappropriate – contravening its description! Take up the ball thread and work along one edge of the foundation row, in a continuous series of chains, joining each chain by its shuttle thread to the foundation. The chains should vary in length, and should have picots on them, in varying positions. Miss a ring of the foundation row occasionally, when working a longer chain.

Turn at the end, and continue in rows of random chains, always joining by the shuttle thread. Check the work as it grows, being careful to keep it flat, and making

Photo 38 *Enlargement of Crescent Collar*

sure that it conforms to the shape of the paper pattern.

The technique can be varied in design by making occasional rings. In practice, it is more convenient to simulate a ring by looping a chain back on itself (joining again to the same picot), than to work a true ring, because it is easier to judge the size of the 'ring' in this way.

Similarly, a Josephine knot can be simulated by working a very tiny chain loop of half stitches.

The technique can be varied further by turning unnecessarily in mid row and proceeding in the opposite direction. This can

be a helpful procedure if at any time the design begins to seem uninteresting. Aim for a contrast of solid areas of tatting against open areas, as well as contrast in the size of the chain loops.

The ready-made fragments are taken into the design as their planned positions are reached. There is no reason why the shuttle and ball in use should not be temporarily abandoned, and further shuttle(s) and ball(s) used. This is often convenient when filling-in between fragments.

A final row is worked all round the outer edge to neaten it. Press the collar carefully under a damp cloth, turning the inner edging underneath.

Dress Trim

Using Coats *Chain Mercer Crochet* No. 20, each motif measures 5.5 cm (2¼ in) in diameter. Four motifs are joined for this trimming but further suggestions for using hexagonal motifs are given in KNOW-HOW 12.

Start at A with a ring of 11ds, p, 4ds, p, 7ds; continue from the diagram as shown.

To join the final ring to the first, use the method for connecting a rosette shown in KNOW-HOW 14 (p. 70).

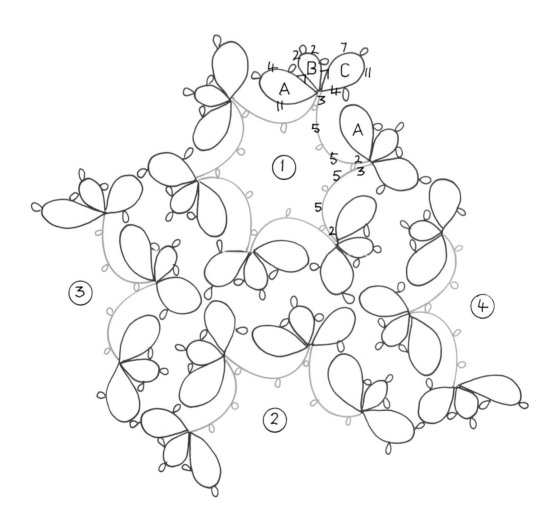

Diag. 34

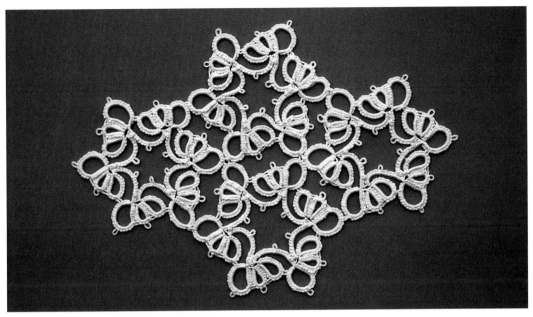

Photo 39 *Dress Trim*

KNOW-HOW 12

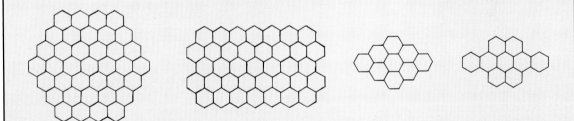

Figs 9(a), (b), (c), & (d) *Designing with hexagons*

To design with hexagonal motifs
Hexagonal or six-sided motifs can be assembled in a varied and interesting number of ways.

Seven motifs form a small flower shape, which can then be expanded in concentric 'circles' to form a larger arrangement (a), which makes an attractive table-cloth. Joined in rows, hexagons can form a rectangular arrangement (b), useful for runners or place mats. Other small arrangements, such as (c) and (d), are useful for dress wear.

Flower Patch

Using Coats *Chain Mercer Crochet* No. 20,
each motif measures 6.5 cm (2½ in) in
diameter.

Start at A with a ring of 7ds, p, 4ds, p, (2ds,
p) twice, 7ds; continue from the diagram as
shown.

To join the final ring to the first, use the
method for connecting a rosette, shown in
KNOW-HOW 14 (p. 70).

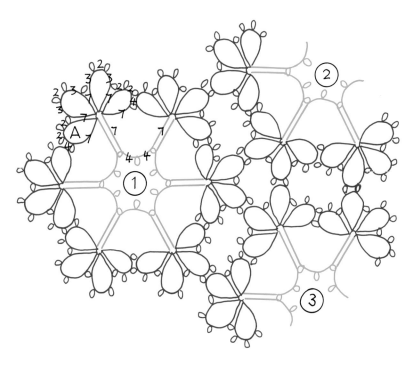

Diag. 35

Photo 40 *Flower Patch*

Flowerpiece

Using Coats *Chain Mercer Crochet* No. 20, the tatting measures 21.5 cm (8½ in) in diameter.

Centre flower motifs

Start at A with a petal ring of 7ds, p, (4ds, p) twice, 7ds; continue from the diagram. All petal rings are the same size, and all small rings are the same size. Final petal ring M joins to its chain by the method given in

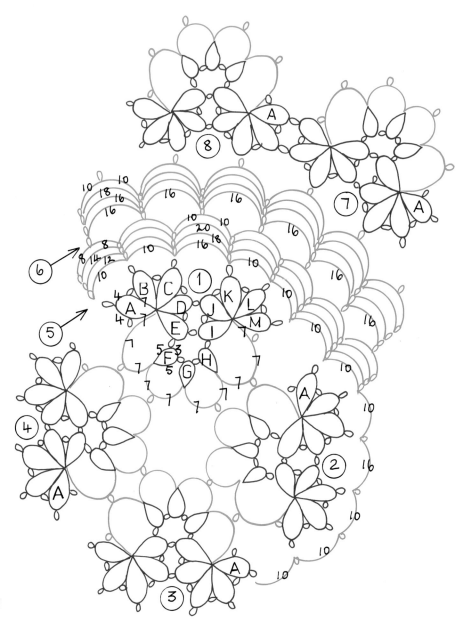

Diag. 36

KNOW-HOW 14 (p. 70) for connecting a rosette.

Join four flower motifs as shown for the centre of the mat.

Chain trails

The chain trails which surround the centre can be started at any free picot. All joins are made with the shuttle thread. Work a minimal picot over each join. Work the first four rounds continuously, then fasten off, and begin again for the following four rounds, which are also worked continuously.

Outer flower motifs

These are twelve in number, worked to match the centre flower motifs. Press the finished mat under a damp cloth.

Photo 41 *Flowerpiece*

Jabot Collar

Using Coats *Chain Mercer Crochet* No. 40, the collar measures 6.5 cm (2½ in) in width; length is adjustable. Matching cuffs can be made from the same pattern.

1st row (inner edging)
Start at A with a ring of (4ds, p) 3 times, 4ds; rw. Continue from the diagram for the length required to the centre front. Work the fall of the jabot to a depth of 16 rings (or as required), and work the second half of the row to match the first half. Turn, and discard the ball thread.

2nd row
Leave a space of approximately 1 cm (⅜ in) on the shuttle thread, and work a tiny ring of 2ds, join to picot of first chain, 2ds. Leave a space as before; tiny ring of 2ds, join to same picot, 2ds. Work across the collar leaving similar spaces throughout, and working two tiny rings into each picot. Where the jabot begins, work only one tiny ring into the joining picot. Turn at the end of the row.

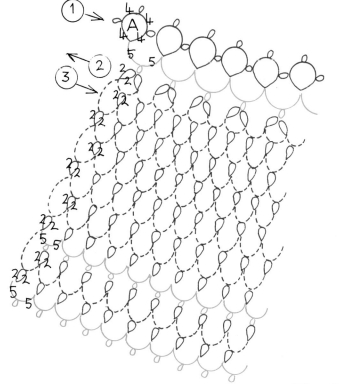

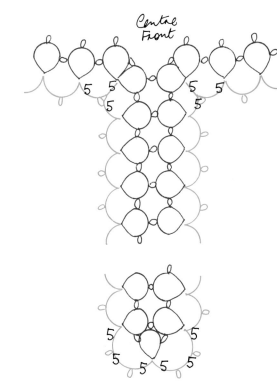

Diag. 37

3rd row
Leave a space as before; tiny ring of 2ds, join to the first space-loop, 2ds.

Continue across the collar, leaving spaces as before, and working one tiny ring into every space-loop. Turn at the end of the row.

Continue from the diagram, picking up the ball thread in order to work the chains of the 8th and 10th rows.

Lightly starch the finished collar.

Photo 42 *Jabot Collar*

Masquerade

Using Coats *Chain Mercer Crochet* No. 20, each motif is 5.5 cm (2¼ in) square.

Start at A with a ring of 8ds, p, 8ds;

continue from the diagram as shown. All chain-to-ring joins are made by the shuttle thread. To complete the motif, join the final chain to the first, using the method for connecting a rosette, shown in KNOW-HOW 14 (p. 70).

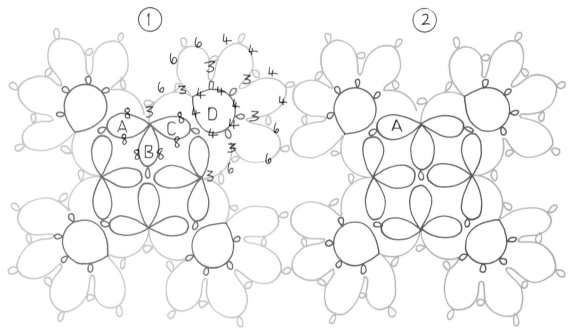

Diag. 38

KNOW-HOW 13

To avoid tying ball and shuttle threads when beginning work
Ideally, it is best to begin with the shuttle wound directly from the ball in a continuous thread (thus negating the need to tie the two ends), but this is not always convenient.

If the thread has had to be cut for

any reason, it is still possible to begin with a 'continuous' thread, by unwinding a length from the shuttle and winding it back on to the ball again. Begin work, and when the break in the ball thread is later reached, join it by either of the methods given in KNOW-HOW 6 (p. 24) or KNOW-HOW 9 (p. 37).

Photo 43 Masquerade

Network

Using Coats *Chain Mercer Crochet* No. 20, the design shown is 19 cm (7½ in) square. It can be enlarged or reduced to any size required, since it is worked diagonally, as a diamond shape.

Start at A with a ring of (6ds, p) 3 times, 6ds.
Ring B of 6ds, join to last picot of previous ring, (3ds, p) 5 times, 3ds.
Chain of 6ds; rw.
Ring C of (3ds, p) 7 times, 3ds.
Chain of 6ds, p, 6ds, join shuttle thread to second picot from the end of ring B, 6ds; rw.

Ring D of (6ds, p) 3 times, 6ds.
Chain of 6ds, p, 6ds, join shuttle thread to picot of chain beneath, 6ds, p, 6ds, join shuttle thread to second picot from the end of ring C, 6ds; rw.
Ring E as ring D.
Chain of (6ds, p, 6ds, join shuttle thread to picot of chain beneath) twice, 6ds, p, 6ds, join shuttle thread to last picot of ring D, 6ds; rw.
Ring F as ring C.

Continue from the diagram(s), always reversing work at the end of a row of chain, before working the ring. Reverse work before and after ring L and all other 'filling' rings.

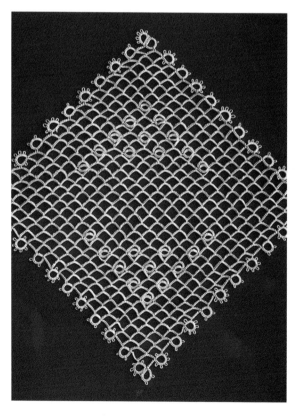

Photo 44 Network

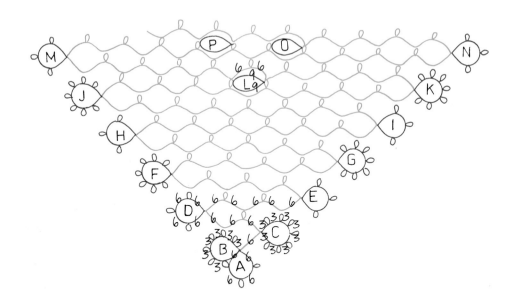

Diag. 39

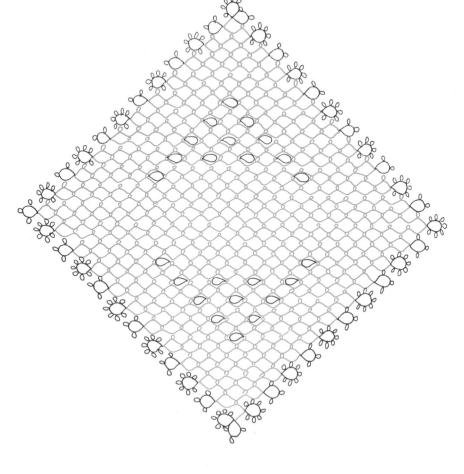

Diag. 40

Patchwork

Using Coats *Chain Mercer Crochet* No. 20 each motif is 5.5 cm (2¼ in) square.

Start at A with a ring of 7ds, p, (4ds, p) twice, 7ds, and continue from the diagram. All large rings are the same size. All small rings are the same size.

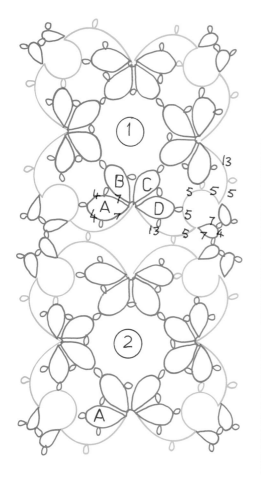

Diag. 41

Photo 45 Patchwork

Polly Flinders

Using Coats *Chain Mercer Crochet* No. 20 each half collar measures 6.5 cm (2½ in) in width, and 19 cm (7½ in) in length along the neck edge.

The diagram shows half the design, and the remainder should be completed to match. The inner edging is worked last.

For all motifs, start at A with a ring of (3ds, p) 5 times, 3ds; rw.

Chain of (4ds, p) twice, 4ds, join shuttle thread to ring A as shown, and continue from the diagram. All rings are the same size but their orientation varies.

In motifs 1, 2 and 3, chains join to rings A, B, D and E by the shuttle thread.

In motif 4, chains join to rings A and B by the shuttle thread.

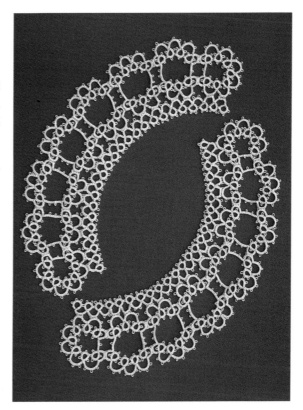

Photo 46 Polly Flinders

Diag. 42

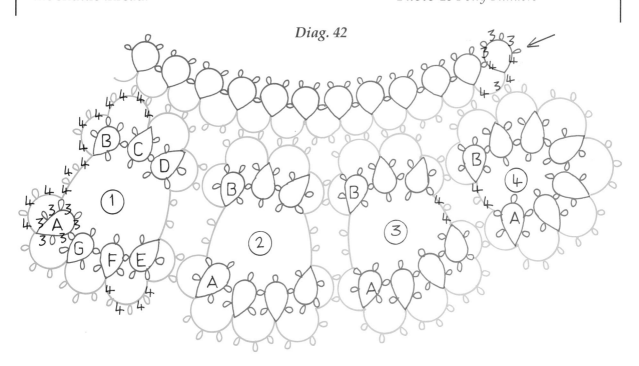

Rosa Frivola

Using Coats *Chain Mercer Crochet* No. 40, the flower measures approximately 6.5 cm (2½ in) in diameter when assembled. Using No. 20, it measures approximately 9 cm (3½ in). Fine floristry wire and floristry tape are needed.

Start at A with a small ring of 16ds; rw, and continue from the diagram. All petal rings are the same size. Work a strip of nine or ten petals, which will curve into a semicircle.

To assemble the flower
Starch the tatting first, then pleat it by running a gathering thread loosely through the small free rings. Roll one end to form the flower's centre and wrap the remaining petals around it. (A certain amount of trial and error may be necessary before a well-shaped flower is achieved.) Sew the base together and insert fine floristry wire through the heart of the flower. Double the wire back and twist to form a stem. Finally, wrap the wire with floristry tape.

Photo 47 Rosa Frivola

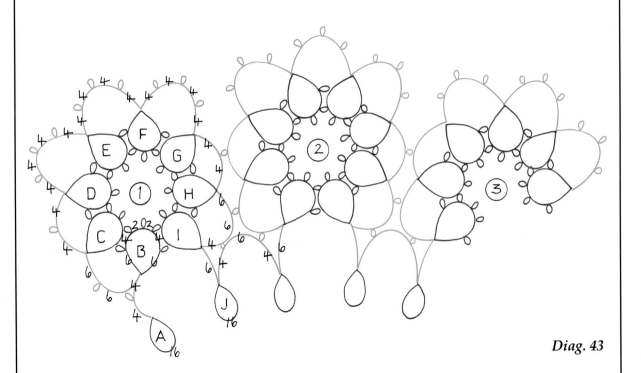

Diag. 43

Rosette Collar

Using Coats *Chain Mercer Crochet* Nos. 20 and 60, each half collar measures 6.5 cm (2½ in) in width, and 19 cm (7½ in) in length at the neck edge; length and curve are adjustable.

Matching cuffs can be made from the same pattern. The double-layered rosettes are worked first.

Double-layered rosette
Using No. 20 crochet cotton, leave an end of approximately 15 cm (6 in) for sewing.

Start at A for the small upper rosette with a ring of (6ds, p) twice, 6ds. Continue from the diagram, joining the first and last rings as explained in KNOW-HOW 14 (p. 70). Tie the threads together at the back of the work to complete the cup-shaped rosette. Leave a minimal space, and start the larger rosette at B with a ring of 8ds, p, (4ds, p) 3 times, 8ds. Continue from the diagram, joining the first and last rings as before. Sew the two rosettes together, so that the smaller is positioned exactly in the centre of the larger.

Main pattern
Using No. 60 crochet cotton, start at C with a ring of 4ds, p, 4ds, join to the larger rosette as shown, 4ds, p, 4ds, rw.

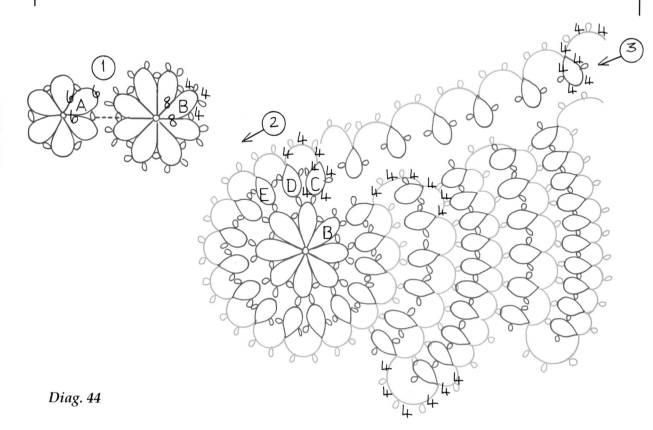

Diag. 44

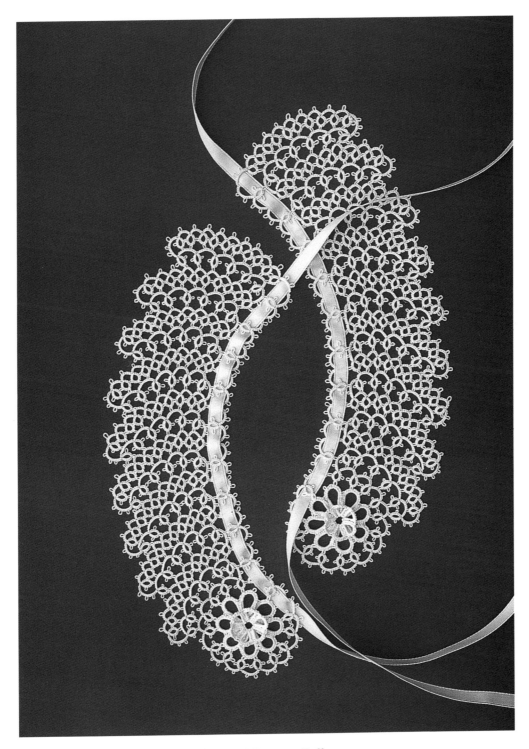

Photo 48 *Rosette Collar*

Continue from the diagram, working around the rosette before starting the rows which form the main pattern. Notice that one picot of the rosette is left unused. When the required number of rows have been worked (ending at the neck edge), do not fasten off, but continue along the side, starting with a chain of (4ds, p) twice, 4ds. Tie the final chain of the edging to the base of ring C to finish.

Second half-collar
Work the double-layered rosette as before, then turn it back to front to begin the main collar. This reversal should enable the two halves to form a matched pair.

Press the main tatting lightly and thread ribbon through the neck edging.

KNOW-HOW 14

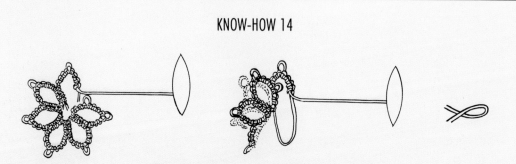

Figs 10(a), (b), & (c) Connecting a rosette

To connect a rosette
When a series of rings is worked to form a rosette, the final connecting join is often a problem as it so often becomes twisted. The following 'rosette join' gives a perfect connection without an unwanted twist. Some tatters describe it as a 'reverse join'.

Hold the work as shown (a), with the final ring upright and incomplete in the hand, and the first ring to the right. Fold the first ring forwards to the left, so that the back of it is facing (b). Give the joining picot of the first ring a half-twist backwards and upwards (c). Insert the hook from the front, complete the join as usual and finish the ring.

With practice, one can flick the picot backwards and upwards with the hook whilst inserting it, but at first it is easier if the two stages are separate.

Photo 49 *Enlargement of Rosette Collar*

Spinning Wheel

Place mat

Using Coats *Chain Mercer Crochet* No. 20, the complete mat measures approximately 30 cm (12 in) in diameter, the edging being 7 cm (2¾ in) in width.

All rings are the same size. Start at A with a ring of (4ds, p) 3 times, 4ds; rw. Continue from the diagram, working a total of 24 repeats of the 2-row pattern (extra repeats are shown in the diagram), and joining the last of these to the loose rings at the beginning. To complete the edging, tie the final edge-chain to the base of first ring A.

To make up

Shrink and lightly press the tatting and the fabric. Using a plate or similar article of diameter to fit the inner edge of the tatting, pencil a circle on the fabric and proceed as explained in KNOW-HOW 15 (p. 75).

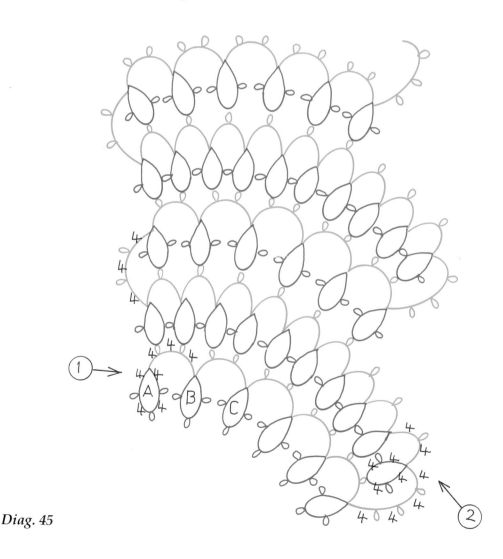

Diag. 45

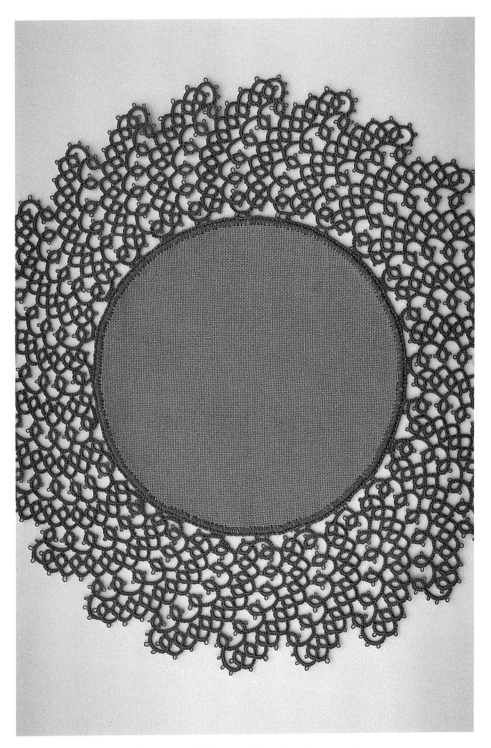

Photo 50 *Spinning Wheel – place mat*

Glass mat

Using Coats *Chain Mercer Crochet* No. 20, the glass mat measures 13 cm (5 in) in diameter.

All rings are the same size. Start at A with a ring of (4ds, p) 3 times, 4ds; rw. Continue from the diagram, working a total of nine 2-row patterns, and joining the last to rings A, B, C and D at the beginning. Fold the work as necessary in order to manipulate these joins, and tie the final chain to the base of the first ring A.

Diag. 46

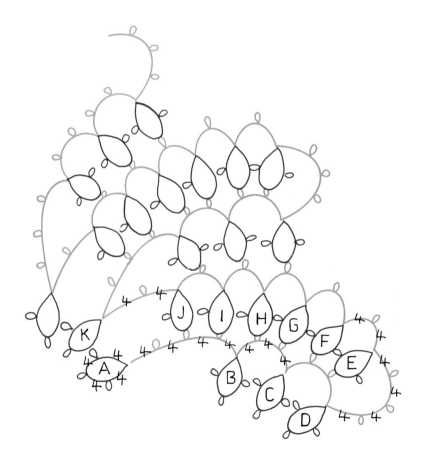

KNOW-HOW 15

To mount a tatted edging on fabric using double crochet

This method is suitable for a curved or straight edge, and the same thread should be used for both the crochet and tatting. The crochet is worked first, then the tatting is overcast to the crochet afterwards, using a finer sewing thread. (A perfectly-matched sewing thread can be obtained by splitting the tatting/crochet thread into single strands.) Alternatively, the tatting can be joined directly to the crochet while the former is being worked, joining with a normal tatted join.

For a straight edge: Roll a narrow double hem, pulling a thread from the fabric at the base of this hem. Working from the same side (which is the back of the fabric), work double crochet over the rolled hem, inserting the hook where the thread was removed.

For a curved edge: Mark the curve with a pencil using a plate or any convenient template. Run a tacking thread along the mark as a stay, in order to prevent stretching. Fold back the fabric once only along the tacking line and work double crochet from the front, inserting the hook through both layers. Cut away excess fabric at the back afterwards.

Photo 51 *Spinning Wheel – glass mat*

Windmills

This design is an interpretation in tatting of a favourite nineteenth-century crochet lace.

Using Coats *Chain Mercer Crochet* No. 20, each motif measures 7 cm (2¾ in) in diameter. See KNOW-HOW 12 (p. 53) for suggestions for assembling the motifs.

Start at A with a ring of 6ds, p, 2ds, p, 6ds;

rw, and work in continuous rounds from the diagram. All picots should be small, and all chain-to-chain joins are made with the shuttle thread. Finish at G, making sure that there are the same number of chains on each of the six sides, on the final round.

When all motifs have been assembled in the form required, work one round of chains on the outer edge, following the general layout of the windmill patterns. Press carefully under a damp cloth.

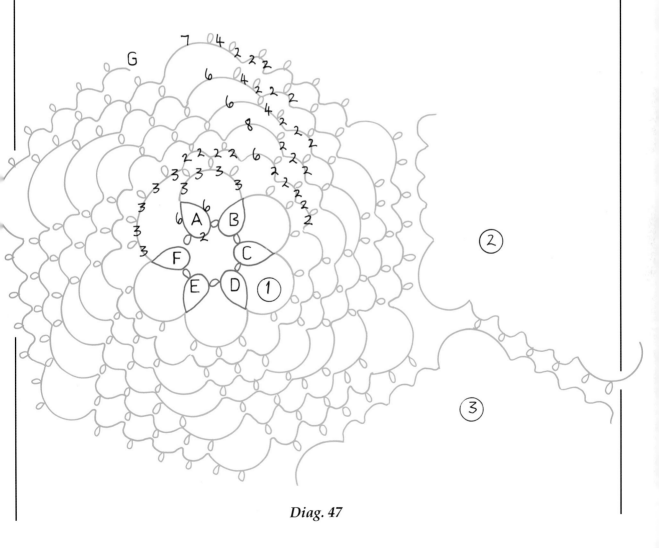

Diag. 47

Photo 52 Windmills

FRAGMENTS
AND
TRIFLES

Anniversary Motif

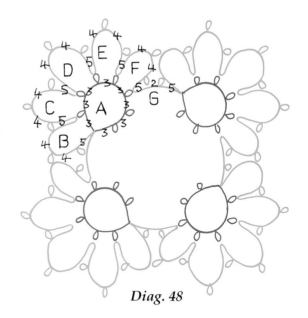

Using Coats *Chain Mercer Crochet* No. 20, the tatting is 5.5 cm (2¼ in) square. This motif matches the Anniversary Braids shown on page 8.

Start at A with a ring of (3ds, p) 7 times, 3ds; rw, and continue from the diagram. All chain-to-ring joins are made with the shuttle thread. All chain-to-chain joins are normal joins. Join final chains F and G to first chain B, and tie chain G to first ring A.

Diag. 48

Photo 53 *Anniversary Motif*

Briar Fragments

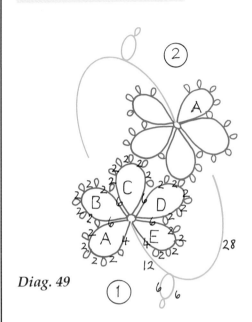

Diag. 49

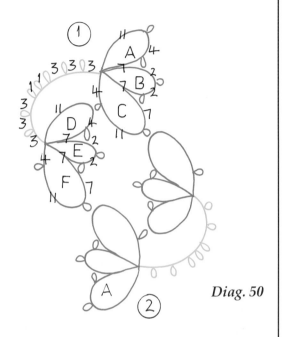

Diag. 50

Using Coats *Chain Mercer Crochet* No. 60, both fragments measure 38 mm (1½ in) in length; using No. 20, both measure 6.5 cm (2½ in).

Left-hand fragment
This is worked in two parts. Using two shuttles wound on a continuous thread, start at A with ring of 4ds, p, (2ds, p) 4 times, 6ds. Continue from the diagram, changing shuttles for the small rings as indicated by the colour. Finish with the long chain, leaving loose ends of approximately 10 cm (4 in) of thread. Work the second part and tie the loose ends of thread to the junctions of petals B and C as shown.

Right-hand fragment[†]
This is also worked in two parts. Start at A with a ring of 11ds, p, 4ds, p, 7ds. Continue from the diagram, fastening off after ring F.

Photo 54 Briar Fragments (see enlargement p. 112)

Photo 55 *Briar Fragment worked in sewing cotton
and mounted in an antique brooch frame*

Bud Fragments

Using Coats *Chain Mercer Crochet* No. 60, the left-hand fragment measures 3 cm (1¼ in) in length; the right-hand fragment measures 28 mm (1⅛ in). Using No. 20, the left-hand fragment measures 4.5 cm (1¾ in) in length; the right-hand fragment measures 38 mm (1½ in).

Left-hand fragment
Start at A with a ring of 8ds, p, 4ds, p, 8ds; rw.
Chain of 10ds, join shuttle thread to last picot of ring; rw.
Chain of 4ds, p, 10ds, join shuttle thread to base of ring, leave a minimal picot over the join, and continue from the diagram.

Right-hand fragment[†]
Start at A with a ring of 14ds, p, 10ds; continue from the diagram as shown.

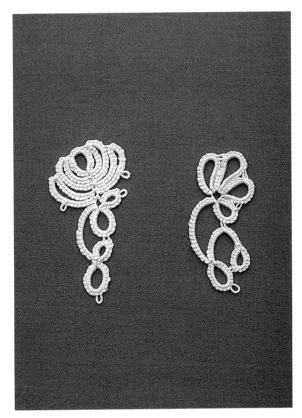

Photo 56 Bud Fragments

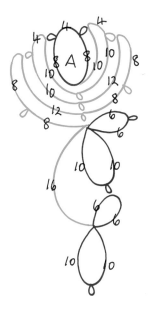

Diag. 51

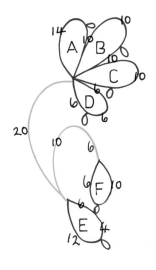

Diag. 52

Coasters

These are an example of random or irregular tatting, sometimes called free tatting.

Using Coats *Chain Mercer Crochet* No. 20, the coasters shown measure approximately 11.5 cm (4½ in) at their widest, but size is adjustable. Both use the same flower fragment as a nucleus on which to base the random tatting.

Start at A with a ring of (3ds, p) 5 times, 3ds; rw. Chain B of 7ds, p, 4ds, p, 3ds, join shuttle thread to next picot of ring A, and continue from the diagram. On ring H, work a long picot and twist it afterwards (*see* KNOW-HOW 10 p. 43). This is shown on the diagram as a straight line.

When the fragment is complete do not fasten off but continue in rounds, working a series of chains, and joining at random with the shuttle thread. The chains should vary in length, and should have picots worked on them in varying positions. Aim for contrast, not only in the size of the chain loops, but in the density of the tatting. The technique can be varied by turning occasionally and proceeding in the opposite direction.

Rings should be included for further contrast, but in practice it is more convenient to make a mock 'ring' in random tatting by looping a chain back on itself – joining twice to the same picot. In this way, the size of a 'ring' can be judged more easily before it is closed. Josephine knots can also be simulated by working very tiny chain loops in half stitches.

The work should be laid on a table from time to time, in order to check that it will lie flat, and that it will eventually reach the required overall shape. If a large mat is preferred, cut a paper pattern as a guide.

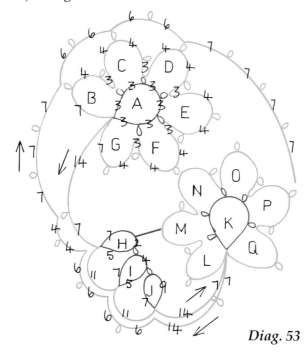

Diag. 53

Photo 57 Coasters

Large Cross

Using DMC *Cordonnet Spécial* No. 40, the cross measures 14 cm (5½ in) in length.

Start at A with a ring of 5ds, p, 10ds, p, 5ds,

and continue from the diagram. To finish, join final ring K to first ring A using the method given in KNOW-HOW 14 (p. 70) for connecting a rosette, and tie the final chain to the base of the first trefoil.

Photo 58 Large Cross

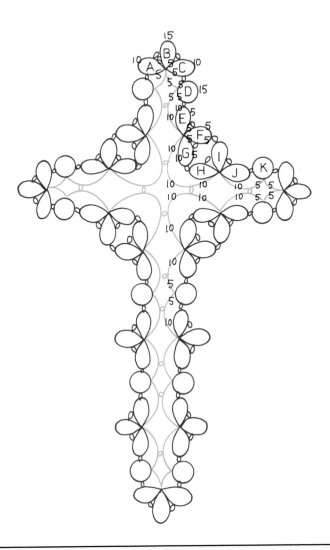

Diag. 54

KNOW-HOW 16

To cut out a mistake
If a mistake in a ring-and-chain design is too disastrous to be unpicked during work, cut away the ring(s), i.e., the shuttle thread, only. The thread from the ball should then remain intact after the shreds of shuttle thread have been extracted from the tatting.

Replace the shuttle thread, using a weaver's knot (KNOW-HOW 8, p. 32) and conceal the ends while continuing work (KNOW-HOW 7, p. 29).

Small Cross

Using DMC *Cordonnet Spécial* No. 40, the cross measures 11 cm (4¼ in) in length.

1st (inner) round
Start at A with a ring of (4ds, p) 3 times,

4ds; rw, and continue from the diagram. All rings are the same size.

2nd (outer) round
This round can be started anywhere. All joins are made with the shuttle thread.

Photo 59 Small Cross

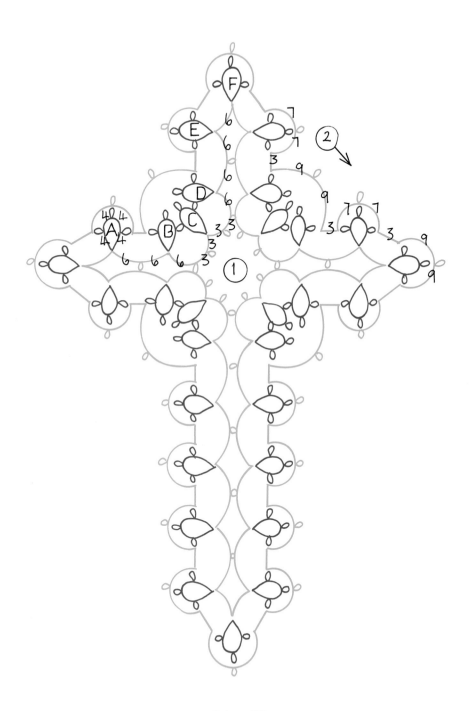

Diag. 55

Faith

Using Coats *Chain Mercer Crochet* No. 20, the tatting is 6.5 cm (2½ in) square.

Start at A with a ring of 5ds, p, (2ds, p) twice, 5ds; rw and continue from the diagram. Rings A to F are all the same size. To join final ring K to ring A at the beginning, use the method for connecting a rosette, shown in KNOW-HOW 14 (p. 70).

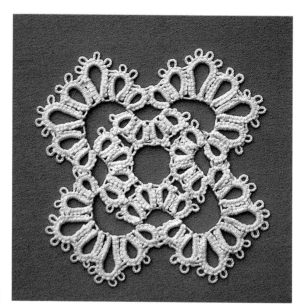

Photo 60 *Faith*

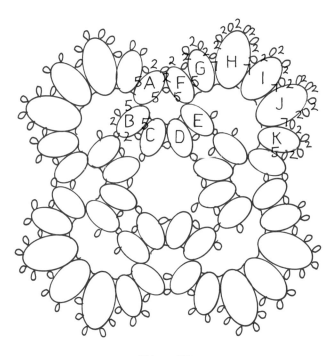

Diag. 56

Flower Fragments

Using Coats *Chain Mercer Crochet* No. 60, the left-hand fragment measures 38 mm (1½ in) in length; the right-hand fragment measures 3 cm (1¼ in). Using No. 20, the left-hand fragment measures 5.5 cm (2¼ in) in length; the right-hand fragment measures 5 cm (2 in).

Left-hand fragment
Start at A with a ring of (3ds, p) 5 times, 3ds; rw.

Chain of 7ds, p, 4ds, p, 3ds, join shuttle thread to next picot of ring, and continue from the diagram. All chain-to-ring joins are made with the shuttle thread. Work a long picot on ring H in order to make a twisted bar (*see* KNOW-HOW 10, p. 43). This is shown as a straight line on the diagram.

Diag. 57

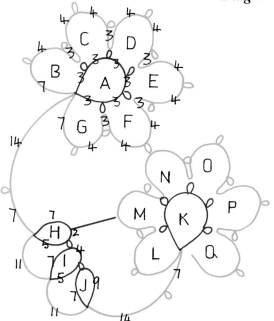

Right-hand fragment
Start at A with a ring of (3ds, p) 7 times, 3ds; rw.

Chain B of 3ds, p, (6ds, p) twice, 3ds, join shuttle thread to next picot of ring, and continue from the diagram. All chain-to-ring joins are made with the shuttle thread. Chains K, L and M are similar to chain J. To join chain M to chain G, use the rosette join shown in KNOW-HOW 14 (p. 70).

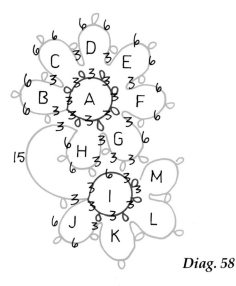

Diag. 58

Photo 61 *Flower Fragments*

Hope

Using Coats *Chain Mercer Crochet* No. 20, the tatting is 5.5 cm (2¼ in) square.

Start at A with a ring of 5ds, p, (2ds, p) twice, 5ds, and continue from the diagram. All rings are worked alike; only their joins and orientation vary.

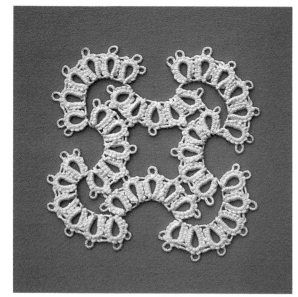

Photo 62 Hope

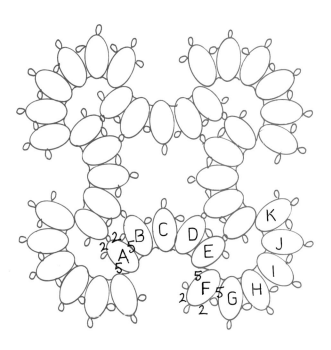

Diag. 59

Posy

Using Coats *Chain Mercer Crochet* No. 20, the tatting measures 6.5 cm (2½ in) in diameter. This design has some complicated joins.

Start at A with a ring of 6ds, p, (4ds, p) twice, 6ds. All rings are worked alike; only their joins and orientation vary. After ring E, take the shuttle thread across the back of the work and join it to the junction of rings C and D. Leave a minimal space, and repeat from ring A, which is joined as shown. Each successive ring E is joined to the previous ring E using the method given in KNOW-HOW 14 (p. 70) for connecting a rosette.

Eight groups form a complete motif. To connect the eighth group to the first, join final ring C to ring A at the beginning (also using the rosette join). Final ring E is joined to first ring E with a normal join, then to 7th ring E with a rosette join. Tie the first end to the junction of final rings C and D.

Photo 63 Posy

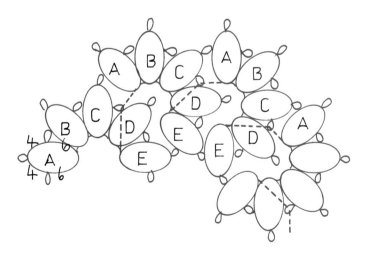

Diag. 60

Queen of Hearts

Using Coats *Chain Mercer Crochet* No. 60, the tatting measures 6.5 cm (2½ in) at its widest.

Start at A with a ring of (4ds, p) twice, 4ds; rw and continue from the diagram as shown. Tie the final chain to the nearest picot of ring A.

Photo 64 Queen of Hearts

Photo 65 *Gift cards displaying Reflection fragment, Ring a Ring O' Roses and Queen of Hearts*

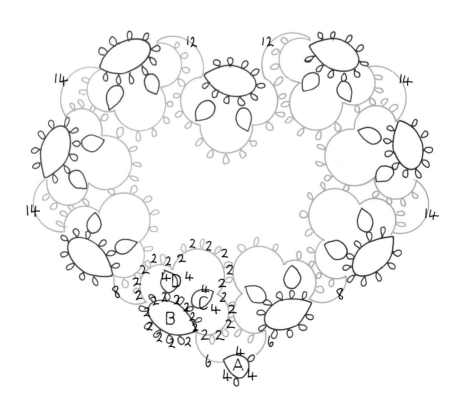

Diag. 61

Reflections

Using Coats *Chain Mercer Crochet* No. 60, the left-hand fragment measures 38 mm (1½ in) in length; the right-hand fragment measures 4.5 cm (1¾ in). Using No. 20, the left-hand fragment measures 5 cm (2 in) in length; the right-hand fragment measures 6.5 cm (2½ in).

Left-hand fragment
This is worked in two parts. Start at A with a ring of 8ds, p, 8ds, and continue from the diagram. Chains join to ring D by the shuttle thread.

Right-hand fragment[†]
This is also worked in two parts. Start at A with a ring of 14ds, p, 5ds, p, 9ds, and continue from the diagram.

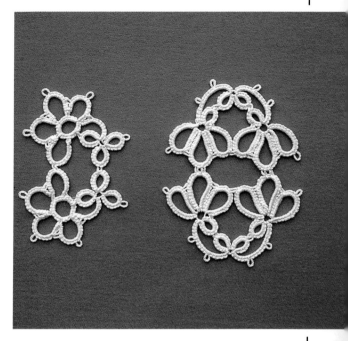

Photo 66 Reflections

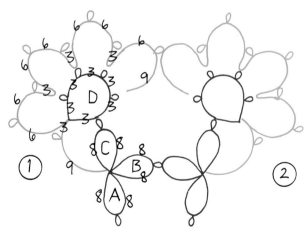

Diag. 62

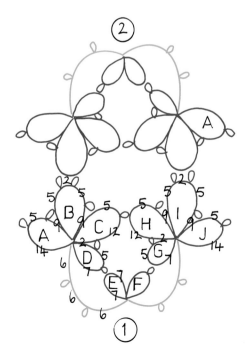

Diag. 63

Ring A Ring O' Roses

The concentric 'triple-ring' was a unit of tatting pioneered by Tina Frauberger of Düsseldorf in the early decades of this century. This design was inspired by her work.

Using Coats *Chain Mercer Crochet* No. 60, the motif measures 7.5 cm (3 in) in diameter. It uses two shuttles wound on a continuous thread, and the motif is worked in a single round.

Start at A with a ring of 14ds, p, 14ds, rw. Chain of (5ds, p) twice, 5ds, join working-shuttle thread to picot of previous ring and leave a tiny picot over the join.

Chain of (5ds, p) twice, 5ds, join working-shuttle thread to base of ring, rw.

Chain of 5ds, join working-shuttle thread to next picot, change shuttles and work ring B. Continue from the diagram, changing shuttles to work the small rings as indicated by the colours. Rings B, C, D, E and F are alike. On ring G, work an extra-large picot. It must be large enough to hold the eight centre rings.

To complete the motif, join final ring E to first ring C, join the following chain to first ring B, and join the final long centre chain to the first centre chain. Tie to base of first ring A to finish.

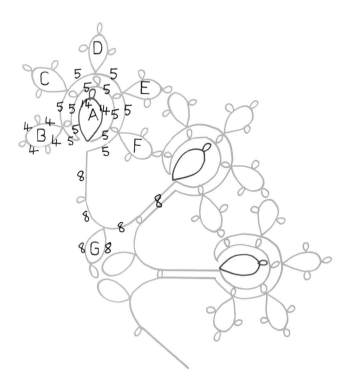

Diag. 64

Photo 67 *Ring a Ring O' Roses*

USES FOR TATTING

Figs 11–16 *Some ideas for the use of tatting on dress wear*

Dress wear

'Laces for a lady' declared Kipling's verse, although the message should not be accepted as authoritative for gentlemen have always worn laces too. It was said that certain highwaymen made it a point of honour to be hanged in theirs.

Tatting can be considered equal to any other form of lace – whether worn by a gentleman or a lady. The town crier of Rochester in Kent wears a fully-tatted jabot and cuffs as part of his official regalia. Ladies, of course, can flaunt their tatting on less-ceremonial occasions.

Tatted edgings, as yard laces, are particularly suited to the country-house style of cotton prints, ruffles and lace typified by the 'Tess of the D'Urbervilles' or dairy-maid look of Laura Ashley fashions. Ruffles at wrist, neck or knee level can be edged easily with tatting. Be lavish, for too sparse an application might leave a would-be admirer wondering whether one had run out of thread or of impetus.

A juxtaposition of tatting, pin tucks and ribbon on a semi-transparent lawn or georgette blouse is an old theme, pure Edwardiana, which can range from the prim to the seductive. Perhaps few tatters nowadays would want to edge their underwear, but one or two have been known to indulge in a tatted garter.

Edgings with a corner design are convenient for square-cut collars and yokes, or for slit hemlines, but they are mainly used for handkerchiefs. Despite the advantages of paper tissues, most tatters still choose to edge handkerchiefs with tatting, because they make such perfect presents.

Many tatted motifs are suitable for appliqué, and as such they can be classed as embroidery rather than lace. Tatted appliqué will often accept the addition of beads or sequins, plus a surround of needle embroidery. Imagine a lush encrustation of tatting on satin, beaded with pearls, as a clutch bag perhaps, or a pill-box hat, or on the bodice of a wedding gown. Conversely, imagine a delicate frosting of tatting on net, sprinkled with confetti-like sequins, gently fluttering, as an overskirt or bridal veil. Size 60 crochet cotton is traditionally used for wedding veils. A more delicate thread might not show to advantage in the final ensemble.

The plainer braid designs work well in embroidery cottons such as pearl cotton or *coton à broder*. The resultant heavier trimmings are quickly made, and are suitable for casual sports or leisure wear, or for adding a 'designer' touch to Chanel-style suits. Embroidery cottons are not as robust as crochet cottons, but they are available in a better range of colours, and will last the life of a T-shirt. These thick cottons ideally need a large shuttle (see TATTING SUPPLIERS p. 118), although for fragments of tatting one can dispense with a shuttle altogether. Simply wind the thread into a figure-of-eight, and secure the bundle with an elastic band.

Tatting for the home

Repeating motifs, such as *Masquerade* (p. 60) or *Flower Patch* (p. 54), can be used for table-cloths and mats of almost any dimension. Tatted edgings with a corner design are useful for table or bed linen, and are usually worked in No. 20 crochet cotton for these purposes. Choose a design without too many ornamental picots if the article in question is intended for frequent laundering, because an excessive number of picots can be tedious to press. While still wet, the tatting should be patted flat with the hands, and not be allowed to dry in a dishevelled state. If pressing is needed, it should be done under a protective cloth.

Tatted braids are useful for trimming lampshades, cushions, curtains, and other soft furnishings, although it is important to choose a thread sufficiently hard-wearing for the intended purpose. Lampshade braids can be splendidly effective if clear glass beads are added, for these will glitter when the lamp is lit. Directions for adding beads to tatting are given in KNOW-HOW 2 (p. 9).

In the kitchen, small fragments of tatting can be dipped, and re-dipped, in a slurry of icing sugar to make unusual cake decorations. Three of the *Bell Flower* (p. 46) motifs, arranged back-to-back, will make an intriguing sugar-coated creation.

Small motifs are popular for mounting under glass paperweights. The still-smaller fragments are favoured for decorating stationery, or for mounting in brooches, pendants, or keyrings. They can also have the additional virtue of being the means of utilising any waste thread remaining on a shuttle after finishing a larger design. If a really tiny specimen of tatting is required, use sewing cotton. Many of the stockists listed (p. 118) also stock a range of mounts, blank cards and other aids for display, in addition to more obvious tatting necessities.

Bookmarks, are always a pleasure to make.

Sometimes it can be difficult to find black thread suitable for tatting (if black is the colour desired). The two *Cross* (pp. 86–9) designs, which are also intended as bookmarks, were made originally in white thread and afterwards dyed by immersion in black ink. (It is advisable to test-dye a scrap of thread first.) These *Cross* designs can have a dual purpose. If worked in richly-coloured embroidery threads, they can form an appliqué basis for ecclesiastical embroidery.

Experimental tatting

Tatting is an old technique, but this does not mean that one is necessarily confined to traditional designs. There is scope for treating tatting as a medium for pictorial work (as a painter would use pigments), or for combining it with other textile constructions in wider ways than may be envisaged.

In general, tatting intended for imaginative experiments in colour and texture seems to be most successful when kept to a basic form of mere rings. Any intricate pattern in the tatting is not of primary importance, being subdued by other considerations. This means that a novice, new to the craft, can express her imagination as easily as an experienced tatter.

Such concepts require a large assortment of threads as a colour palette, and since, sadly, crochet cottons are just not available in anything like the spectrum required, one either has to amass a wide assortment of embroidery threads, or has to resort to fabric dyes and paints. High-gloss threads, such as rayon knitting yarns, are useful,

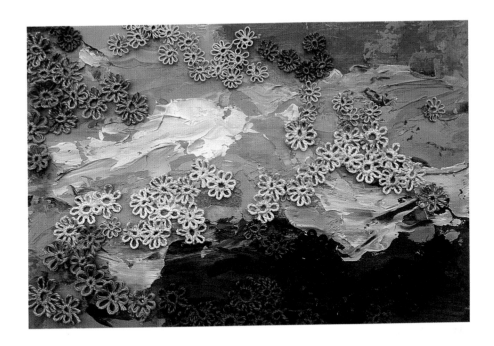

Photo 68 Landscape – tatting with pearl cottons and other embroidery threads combined with impasto oil paint

Photo 69 Meadow – tatting with pearl cottons and other embroidery threads combined with impasto oil paint

Photo 70 *Lilac – tatting with pearl cottons and other embroidery threads plus oil paint (see enlargement on back cover)*

Photo 71 *Collage using a contrast of matt and glossy threads*

Photo 72 Tatting and knitting

since a contrast of matt and glossy threads can add extra interest.

You can achieve pictorial designs by combining simple tatted rings with impasto oil paint (*see* p. 101). The rings are embedded in the paint before it has dried. Alternatively, you can combine tatted rings with very thin oil paint, by gluing the tatting on afterwards with PVA adhesive.

Another idea (*see* opposite) is to make a collage of different nets, threads and clustered rings, assembled with the aid of PVA adhesive. To keep it clean it is best mounted under glass. There are other possibilities for combining tatting with net; for instance, you could use embroidery techniques, such as couching, instead of adhesive; or combine tatting with tambouring – leaving long ends of thread on the rings, to be worked ornamentally through the net with a tambour hook.

The possibilities of using tatting with different textile crafts have not yet been fully exploited. Tatting and fine crochet are old companions, as are tatting and needlepoint lace. It is obvious that tatting can be combined with all sorts of embroidery crafts, but it can also be used in a very simple way in conjunction with knitting. In the photograph above plain tatted rings were added to reversed stocking-stitch in such a way that they almost seem to be an extension of the slubbed knitting yarn. Long ends of thread left on these rings were afterwards hooked through to the back of the work where they were tied. Similarly, hand-woven fabrics can be embossed with tatted rings, their long ends being taken into the warp during the process of weaving.

Random or free tatting, introduced on pages 50 and 84, can be considered almost as a graphic art technique, the continuous chains being a medium for drawing. The examples shown in the pattern pages are functional items, but there is no reason why the general principles of random tatting should not be allowed a wider range and be applied to pictorial projects.

BASIC TECHNIQUES

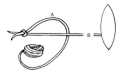

Fig. 17 *Using different colours for the ball and shuttle threads, tie them together*

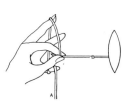

Fig. 18 *Grip the knot. Wrap ball thread A over the left hand and round the little finger*

Fig. 19 *Make a loop with shuttle thread B as shown and pass the shuttle upwards under A and through loop B*

Fig. 20(a) *Thread B now forms a loop on straight thread A*

Fig. 20(b) *'Transfer' the loop by tugging the shuttle sharply while dropping the middle finger to slacken A. Thread A now forms a loop on straight thread B, and becomes a half stitch*

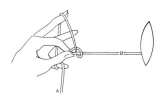

Fig. 21 *Slide the half stitch up next to the knot by raising the middle finger. Hold the half stitch firmly in place with the thumb*

Fig. 22 *Pass the shuttle downwards under A and over B*

Fig. 23(a) *Thread B now forms a loop on straight thread A*

Fig. 23(b) *'Transfer' the loop as in 20(b). Thread A now forms a loop on straight thread B, and becomes a second half stitch*

Fig. 24 *The two halves pair to form a double stitch*

Fig. 25 A series of double stitches form a chain. To make a picot, leave a small space between the double stitches, then slide them together to close the space

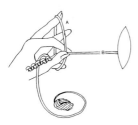

Fig. 26 To make a ring, drop the ball thread and wrap the shuttle thread completely around the left hand in a circle. A and B are now different parts of the same thread. Work a series of double stitches as before. All stitches should slide easily on thread B. As the circle contracts, stretch the fingers to enlarge it

Fig. 27 To close and complete the ring, slip it off the fingers and gently pull the shuttle thread. If the ring will not close, then the 'transfer' stages, 20(b) and 23(b), have been omitted or incorrectly worked

Fig. 28 To join rings and/or chains in tatting, insert a hook into a previously worked picot and draw thread A through. Pass the shuttle through the loop made by A

Fig. 29 Tighten and adjust A so that it slides on B. This join counts as a half stitch. Follow it with a second half stitch to simulate a double stitch

Fig. 30 To work a series of rings and chains, reverse work (turning the tatting upside-down in the hands) after completing each ring and each chain. Use the shuttle thread only for the rings, and both ball and shuttle threads for the chains

Fig. 31 A Josephine knot is a tiny ring of half stitches

Fig. 32 To work a Josephine knot on a chain, wind thread A on to a second shuttle before commencing the tatting

DICTIONARY OF TERMS

English	French	German
tatting/shuttle lace	frivolité	Schiffchenspitze
shuttle	navette	Schiffchen
ring	anneau/boucle	Ring
chain	arceau/chaine	Bogen
picot	picot	Pikot/Öse
double stitch/knot	noeud double	Doppelknoten
half stitch/knot	demi noeud/noeud simple	Halbknoten
first half stitch	noeud endroit	Rechtsknoten
second half stitch	noeud envers	Linksknoten
Josephine knot	picot Joséphine	Josephinen/Muschenknoten
reverse work	(re)tournez l'ouvrage	Arbeit wenden
join	raccordez	anschliessen/verbinden
close	fermez	zusammenziehen
thread	fil	Faden

Dutch	Italian	Spanish	Swedish
frivolité	chiacchierino/occhi	encaje de lanzaderas	orkidé/frivolitets
spoel	navetta	lanzadera	skyttel
ring	anello	anillo	ring
boog	arca	arco	båge
pikot/lusje	pippiolini	baguilla	picot
dubbele knoop	punto/nodo	punto/nudo doble	dubbelknut
halve knoop	mezzo nodo		
eerste helft			
tweede helft		nudo derecho	
halve boog	nodo Guiseppina	nudo izquierdo	
kern werk	voltare il lavoro	vuelta a la labor	vänd arbetet
verbinden	attaccare	enganchar	sammanfoga/fäst
sluiten	chuidere	cerrar	drar ihop/tillsluta
draad	filo	hilo	tråd

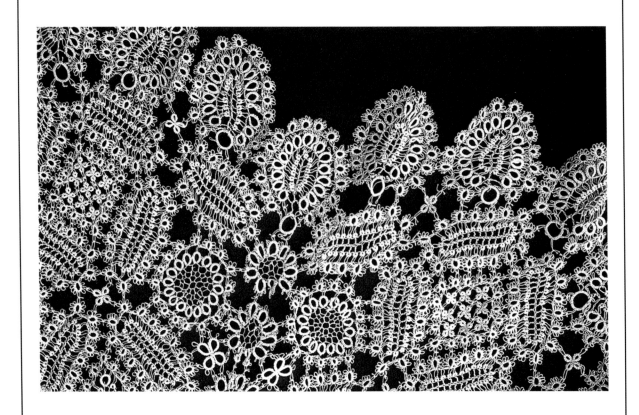

Photo 73 *Close-up of the parasol cover shown in* ***Photo1.***

All rings are either tied or sewn together. Some motifs include needlepoint lace fillings.

(see page vi for Photo 75)

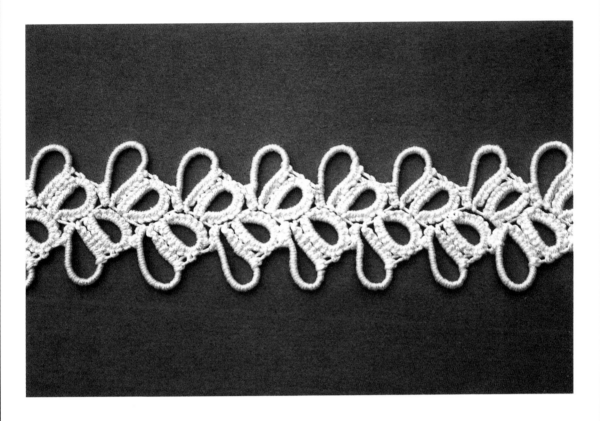

Photo 75 *Enlargement of Lupins (see p. 19)*

Photo 76 *Enlargement of Onion Skins (see p. 24)*

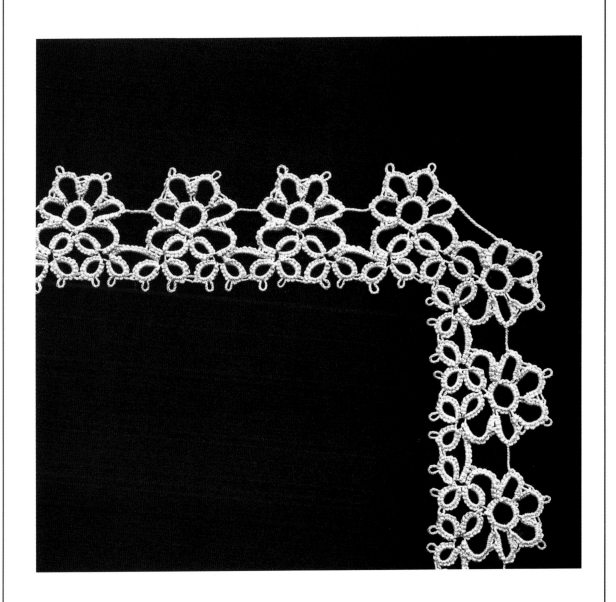

Photo 77 *Enlargement of Wallflowers (see p. 44)*

Photo 78 *Enlargement of Briar Fragments (see p. 81)*

INDEX